Alexander Wedderburn

Report on the extent and character of food and drug

adulteration

Alexander Wedderburn

Report on the extent and character of food and drug adulteration

ISBN/EAN: 9783337201050

Printed in Europe, USA, Canada, Australia, Japan

Cover: Foto ©Andreas Hilbeck / pixelio.de

More available books at **www.hansebooks.com**

BULLETIN No. 41

U. S. DEPARTMENT OF AGRICULTURE

DIVISION OF CHEMISTRY

REPORT

ON THE

EXTENT AND CHARACTER

OF

FOOD AND DRUG ADULTERATION

BY

ALEX. J. WEDDERBURN

SPECIAL AGENT

PUBLISHED BY ORDER OF CONGRESS
(Act approved August 8, 1894)

WASHINGTON
GOVERNMENT PRINTING OFFICE
1894

LETTER OF TRANSMITTAL.

U. S. Department of Agriculture,
Division of Chemistry,
Washington, D. C., May 10, 1891.

Sir: I have the honor to present herewith, at your request, the manuscript, prepared by Mr. A. J. Wedderburn. special agent, embracing his third report on the extent and character of adulterations of food and drugs.

Very respectfully,

H. W. Wiley,
Chief of the Division of Chemistry.

Hon. J. Sterling Morton,
Secretary.

LETTER OF SUBMITTAL.

U. S. DEPARTMENT OF AGRICULTURE,
DIVISION OF CHEMISTRY,
Washington, D. C., July 1, 1894.

SIR: In compliance with my commission as special agent to examine into the extent and character of food and drug adulterations, I have the honor to submit the following report. Increased interest in this subject, as shown by the great increase in correspondence, has compelled me to go over the old ground to a considerable extent, but I believe that new and interesting matter will be found herein. The character of my commission did not authorize investigation of the scientific phases of the subject which are so ably covered in the various parts of Bulletin No. 13, issued under your direction.

Very respectfully,

ALEX. J. WEDDERBURN,
Special Agent.

Dr. H. W. WILEY,
Chemist of the U. S. Department of Agriculture.

CONTENTS.

PREFATORY NOTE.

On the appointment of Mr. A. J. Wedderburn as special agent of the Department, a circular approved by the Assistant Secretary of Agriculture was sent to about 9,000 druggists and to all the officers and members of State pharmaceutical and dairy associations whose addresses could be obtained. The text of this circular was as follows:

> Please furnish me with any information that you may have in relation to the use of pepsin or black pepsin in (so-called) butter-making. I should be glad to learn also anything in relation to any other butter and cheese adulterants and to obtain any reliable data concerning the adulteration of children's foods, dairy and pharmaceutical preparations. I inclose franked envelope for reply.
>
> Please furnish me the names and addresses which you may know of any State or municipal officials charged with executing the laws relating to the adulteration of foods and drugs, also the names of officers or members of the pharmaceutical associations and dairy organizations in your State, and oblige.

Many replies were received to this circular. Mr. Wedderburn during his service as special agent classified and abstracted the greater number of them, but the material was not entirely put in shape for publication. By instructions of the Secretary of Agriculture I have endeavored to complete this work and prepare the material for transmittal. The details of the work and the use to be made of the material collected were left entirely to the judgment of the special agent.

All the information in regard to the use of black pepsin has been omitted for the reason that the subject is fully discussed in Farmers' Bulletin No. 12.

The Chief of the Division of Chemistry does not hold himself in any way responsible for the opinions of the correspondents quoted in the selections made for publication, nor for all the conclusions arrived at by the compiler. In fact, there are many cases in which these opinions are without doubt erroneous, as where one correspondent describes flour as largely adulterated with "earth from the South," and another asserts that the sugars of commerce are also adulterated, and where a third affirms that artificial eggs are manufactured.

The information which is here presented illustrates the attitude of the public mind to the problem of adulteration. It is hardly necessary

9

to call attention here to the fact that the public ideas of adulteration of food are in many cases very much exaggerated, and this, perhaps, is the cause of the many extravagant assertions which are made.

The arrangement of the material in this bulletin was a matter of careful consideration, and it was deemed best to make as few changes in the original matter as were compatible with a proper classification of the data at hand. The changes, furthermore, made by me in the manuscript are only such as have helped to a better statement of the facts or to correct errors overlooked by the compiler.

H. W. WILEY,
Chief of the Division of Chemistry.

REPORT ON THE EXTENT AND CHARACTER OF FOOD AND DRUG ADULTERATION.

By Alex. J. Wedderburn.

INTRODUCTORY.

The discussion of food adulteration in this country and the consequent agitation of the subject have drawn the attention of foreigners to the fact that adulteration exists among us to a greater or less degree, and the result is that the foreign competitors of our manufacturers of food products have used the fact to their own advantage, and America to-day occupies the unenviable position of being one of the very few countries of Christendom that fail to require by law the proper branding of their manufactured food and drugs. Whether such requirements would accomplish the desired result is beyond the power of anyone to say, but the evil would no doubt be mitigated by wholesome legislation, and this belief is sustained by the results of the food laws of England and other foreign countries, as well as of the various States. The concurrent testimony of State officials charged with the enforcement of State and local laws is that a national law is necessary to secure the proper enforcement of State laws. No well-informed constitutional lawyer will dispute the fact that so long as the " original-package" decision stands as law, it will be impossible for any State, no matter how stringent its laws, or how efficient its officers, to fully execute them. If this be true, and the fact be established that adulterations exist to any considerable extent or that they are harmful to health, morals, or industry, and the writer believes the facts sustain the assertion, then the need for a Federal law is imperative. There can be no doubt that the effort to purge the country of this crime is doing good and aids in keeping down the adulteration of the products we consume, but each year brings to light new articles in which some intelligent "artist" has discerned a method to improve the profit if not the quality of the article sold.

That almost every article of food and drug used in our country is adulterated to a greater or less extent is proved most conclusively by a vast amount of information gathered upon the subject by the Division of Chemistry of the Department of Agriculture, and referred to

the writer for compilation and report. The extent of these sophistications can be truthfully said to be as broad as the continent.

Their character, however, is such as to injure the pocket rather than
the health. The general character of food adulterations is principally
commercial fraud, and the extent of criminal or poisonous adulterations in food is so limited as to amount to but a bagatelle in the
immense sum of the products consumed. I am convinced that a
large proportion of poisonous adulterations arises from carelessness
and ignorance, rather than from any desire to injure the customer to
whom sale is made. But ignorance is no excuse for the wholesale
destruction of life by the addition of poisonous pigments to many articles of food, especially confectionery, cream, and like articles. It would
occupy too much space to show the numerous cases of poisoning from
eating cream, cakes, candies, cheese, pickles, canned goods, etc., and
would add little value to this report; but the fact that such occurrences
are not only common but frequent shows the existence of an evil that
demands the strictest remedial legislation possible.

The existence of adulterations is conclusively proved in the pages
of Bulletins Nos. 13 (parts 1 to 8), 25, and 32, issued by the Division
of Chemistry of the Department of Agriculture; by every report of
State officials, where such exist; by testimony from every State where
investigations have been set on foot by pharmaceutical or pure-food
associations; by the testimony herewith submitted from every quarter
of this country, and by the admissions of the adulterators themselves.

That adulteration is general and increasing is proved in the following
pages, as is also the fact that no kind of food, drugs, or liquors is free
from the finishing touches of the manipulators. It may be, therefore,
concluded that the practice is general and the character principally
fraudulent, with but occasional criminal additions, the latter, however,
too frequently causing loss of life and health. Ignorance and vice go
hand in hand in their destructive game, yet, whether the intent be criminal and vicious, or simply fraudulent, the result is the same, and the
people suffer and will continue to suffer until the strong hand of Federal
law steps in to supplement and support the action of the States.

As to the harmfulness of these practices, one has but to read the
results of coroners' inquests, in all sections of the Union, to determine
for himself that question. When illness and death occur from eating
or drinking some attractive and beautifully prepared article of food,
the fact that harm exists is proved. In a previous report I have shown
that death resulted from the use of chrome yellow not only to the customer, but also to the vendor and members of his family. This did not
of necessity prove the man who used and sold the article a knave, but
it proved him a fool. Now, to prevent a repetition of such occurrences,
the law should compel the man who manufactured the coloring matter
to brand it so that even the most ignorant could distinguish its harmful qualities, and thereby at least restrict the use of such articles.

In such cases ignorance should be no excuse for crimes perpetrated for the purpose of gain. The murder of one innocent, like the child in Brooklyn, who was killed by eating a "greened" pickle, was more of a crime against human rights than all the restrictive laws that could be put upon the Federal statutes. It is generally conceded by my correspondents that a Federal law will secure prompt action on the part of those States which have failed to take action in this matter, and thus lessen the chances for like occurrences.

In the case of drugs the extraction of their strength, their manufacture in a careless manner, or the substitution of an inferior article, are other matters entirely, and are not only crimes against the pocket, but against health and life. Nearly all of the States, recognizing the necessity for the prevention of crimes of this character, have stringent pharmacy laws, the enforcement of which is not only beneficial to the public but also of untold value to the reputable druggist, who is as anxious to prevent fraud as anyone.

The reports of the various pharmaceutical associations of the country show that the members are earnest advocates of pure drugs, and yet the reports of their various committees on deterioration and adulteration all show the existence to a greater or less extent of adulterations. Letters from leading men in the business say that until the Federal Government enacts a law which will prevent the shipment of articles from one State to another unless properly branded, State laws to prevent the sale of such articles must of necessity prove ineffective.

Adulterations in our food, our drugs, and drinks exist to a very great extent in every State. In previous bulletins—Nos. 25 and 32—the writer has claimed, from data at hand, that the extent of adulteration is not less than 15 per cent, and he is still convinced that this is rather below than above the mark. Of this amount probably only 2 per cent is of an injurious character to health, but when we remember that to furnish 65,000,000 people with food, drink, and drugs costs not less than $6,760,000,000 (allowing the average cost per capita to be only $2 per week), we find by calculation that the amount of adulteration reaches the immense sum of $1,014,000,000 annually, and as the population increases each year so will increase this constant drain upon the resources of the people. It may be said that a large proportion of this is simply a deterioration, and that the purchaser gets value for his money and is benefited by the reduced price. Were this true, the loss still falls upon the producer of the genuine article, and it must be recollected that at least 2 per cent of the whole is of a character deleterious to health, which amounts to the sum of $135,200,000 as the annual amount paid by the American people for having their lives taken or their health injured.

No one attempts to controvert the assertion that when a purchaser tries to buy an article, and is ready to pay for it the price asked, he should be given that article and not a substitute, even if the substitute be better, unless its true character be explained. It is claimed by the vendor of adulterated goods that the demand for cheap goods causes the supply; that the desire to get something for nothing ends in compelling sophistications. Admitting the justice of such a line of argument, it only goes to show the utter disregard people have for their own comfort and pockets, and their absolute ignorance upon matters relating to their health. People who take it for granted that what they eat is all right will take very great care about selecting their shoes and clothes. Under such circumstances, and believing that there exists no more serious or exhaustive drain upon the resources of the people than the adulteration of their food and drug products, I take it that the Federal Government should enact a law of such a character as to prevent the transportation of misbranded, poisonous, or deleterious food and drug products from one State or Territory into another, not interfering with the police powers of the States. This being done, the various State laws would become effective, and by systematic effort on the part of officials or honest dealers and manufacturers, adulterations would be reduced to a minimum and millions of dollars saved annually to the country.

Fortunately most of these adulterations are commercial frauds only, but these in themselves produce others and degrade the tone of morality. They would be rejected by the majority of dealers and manufacturers if the law enabled them to compete with dishonesty, but so long as no restriction is placed upon the evil-doer so long will he attempt to make money by swindling his fellows, and naturally the more honest man, finding his business ruined by the pirate, without chance for redress or relief, drifts into the same channel and becomes a party to the crime by adopting the methods and practices of the rogue.

The law should not be made to discriminate against one class of manufacturers or producers at the expense of another, equality before the law being the fundamental principle of our Government; but as the necessity for law exists only to insure the life, liberty, and happiness of our people, its province is undoubtedly to protect the weak and restrain the strong, especially when by misrepresentation frauds are put upon the people in the essentials of life and health, and the products of honest manufacture and agriculture are debased, as is done when a food or drug product is sold under a misleading brand, or for something which it is not, thereby reducing the value of the real product. In many cases the masquerader usurps the market and destroys the genuine article. Honest business is thus demoralized, and when our products seek a foreign market they are met by the foreign inspector, who at once discovers the fraud and advertises to the world our people as a set of swindlers, and our Government as the abetter and aider in the crime, because it fails to do as all other civilized and Christian lands do, viz, see that the products sold to the people are branded true to name. Repeated instances of exposure of fraud in

American food products have been made in Europe and South America. The result has been to greatly restrict trade with our neighbors—trade essential to the material prosperity of our agricultural interests. Proof of this interference with American exports is ample, and data could be secured to fill a volume, but I deem such matter unnecessary. I quote, however, from the Baltimore Sun the following extract, contained in an article written for that paper by Prof. William P. Tonry, one of the most eminent analytical chemists of the country, which goes to show what effect adulteration has in shutting out our commerce from the nations of the world in even so comparatively insignificant an article as candy:

As to the commercial results of the adulteration of candies, a confectioner whose reputation for absolutely pure confectionery is unquestioned told me that his sales per annum did amount to $96,000, of which about $40,000 were export trade to South American, West Indian, and Mexican ports. Philadelphia, New York, and Boston houses entered the same field and, placing their goods at a lower figure, did for a short time supply a good article, but soon replaced it by the adulterated. The result was that the customer refused to have the American article at any price, and the local Spanish dealers now send to Barcelona, Spain, for a pure candy. The less discriminating consumers here give preference to adulterated articles, which can be purchased cheaper, and thus $40,000 export trade and $50,000 home trade are the penalty one house alone has had to pay for adherence to unadulterated goods, while the commercial reputation of the United States has been very much depreciated, if not entirely blasted.

It is claimed that the Federal Government has no right to interfere with what a man buys or sells, no right to interfere with what he eats or drinks, or to bother as to whether he deceive his customer or not—that all such questions are to be decided by the several States and the individuals themselves. It may be true that the Government has no right to interfere in these matters, but when, from the very nature of the Constitution, Congress alone can enable the States to enforce their own laws, such legislation should be enacted as will permit them to make effective laws enacted by their legislatures. Congress alone has power to regulate commerce between the States, and until it enacts laws providing for the prevention of the transportation from one State into another of the adulterated food and drug products no State law can be enforced.

If any foreign Government were to interfere with the business rights of our people the Federal Government would retaliate; but in the case of an adulteration the Federal Government, it is claimed, has no right to interfere, and the honest, industrious citizen is frozen out of business while the scamp is permitted to continue his nefarious and unholy practices. Counterfeiters of money are restrained, violators of the revenue laws are held in check, pirates are summarily disposed of, but those who counterfeit food and drugs, violate the various State laws, and bring dishonor on the country by pirating and sailing under the black flag of destruction to honest trade are permitted to continue in their outrageous practices for lack of a Federal law permitting the States to enforce their statutes.

Many of the misbranded goods are, doubtless, as good as the articles which they seek to supplant; in some cases, probably, they are superior. Would it not be better for the interests of all concerned to brand them true to name, and for the protection of the purchasers at home and abroad, as well as those manufacturers who prefer to do a legitimate business (by far the great majority), for the National Government to enact such remedial legislation as will prevent interstate or foreign traffic in misbranded food and drug products. The cost of executing such a law need not be immoderate, and should be borne by the manufacturers of food and drug products. A small registration fee, say $10, on each manufacturer (not each article) would fully cover all the cost, and the result would be of such a beneficial character as to soon receive the indorsement of all parties interested. One official for each State, or, at the outside, two, to coöperate with the State officials, would be all that would be needed to prevent violations of the law, and reduce adulteration appreciably, as all reputable dealers would be only too glad to assist in preventing a competitor from underselling them by means of fraudulent brands. That any law can prevent crime is, of course, not to be expected, but in the case of a national food and drug adulteration law the assistance rendered by honest manufacturers and dealers and the State officials would, after one or two convictions, be so convincing as to materially reduce the desire to sell fraudulent goods. Speaking of the necessity for supervision of the food and drug products, Dr. R. C. Kedzie, in an argument before the Michigan legislature, said:

But the fact that there is such an official at work would do much to infuse a healthy tone of honesty among manufacturers and keep such poor stuff out of our State. The admonition, "There's a chiel amang ye takin' notes, and faith he'll prent 'em," will prove a healthy tonic for public morals. A fraud may make light of any threat of exposure, but it fears nothing so much as the light. It requires strong pressure to gain its consent to be exposed in the public press.

Without further comment I submit a revised list of adulterants, various comments from State officials, extracts from official reports, newspapers, chemists, and other correspondents, and would direct special attention to the lax provisions for enforcing the statutes in most of the States. These subjects have been collected under appropriate headings. It would be impossible to reproduce the hundreds of letters or all the data that have been secured, or to publicly acknowledge the assistance rendered me by many gentlemen who have kindly and promptly furnished important information, but I desire to express to each my thanks for prompt and courteous assistance. In the following extracts, selected from many similar letters, will be found as fair an exhibit of the views upon the question of food and drug adulterations as could possibly be submitted. The preponderance of opinion shows the feeling of the great mass of the people upon this subject. All kinds and classes, with wonderful unanimity, join in testifying as to adulteration. This being the case, we are led to conclude that adulteration is general. The letters presented show the character of these sophistications to be principally of a harmless (to health but not to the pocket) character. In many instances, however, poisons and injurious adulterants are used. The classification by States seems to be the best and easiest method of arrangement, and has, therefore, been selected. It will be seen that letters, extracts, reports, etc., have been received from many States showing that no part of the country is free from this nefarious practice. It will be observed that nearly all the State officials and representative tradesmen who touch on the subject unite in urging the passage of a national food and drug law for the protection of legitimate industry and our interstate and foreign commerce, as well as the public health.

3183—No. 41——2

OPINIONS OF STATE AND MUNICIPAL OFFICERS AND OTHERS REGARDING THE ADULTERATION OF FOOD AND DRUGS.

ALABAMA.

From Alphonse L. Stollenwerck, of the Newman & Stollenwerck Drug Company, Birmingham, Ala.:

I have no data of adulteration of drugs and food products, for the reason that I never took the trouble to make memoranda. I have no doubt but that I could gather up quite a number of adulterated foods and drugs. We have no preventive laws in this State. We have an Alabama State pharmacy law, which pertains only to the licensing of pharmacists. In 1881 I organized a county pharmaceutical association in Jefferson County, and the following year organized the Alabama State pharmaceutical association, of which I was the president for two years. As the president of this association, I framed the present pharmacy law. We have never been able to pass a law pertaining to adulteration of drugs, medicines, and foods. I think a law governing these articles if properly enforced would be of great material good to the community at large. I think the manufacturers of patent and proprietary medicines and of food products are allowed entirely too much latitude, inasmuch as unscrupulous manufacturers put upon the market and advertise preparations not only devoid of medicinal properties but which are absolutely injurious to the consumer.

From H. N. Rosser, health officer, Birmingham, Jefferson County, Ala.:

In my opinion a national law requiring the proper labeling of drugs and groceries in packages as to quality and quantity is a "consummation devoutly to be wished," as many of the pharmaceutical preparations sent to this market are not of the quality specified on the labels, and many of our canned groceries are short in weight, of inferior quality, and often adulterated. Our city code has nothing in it in regard to adulterations, and we have no system of inspection in Alabama.

From N. T. Lupton, State chemist, Agricultural and Mechanical College, Auburn, Ala.:

Annotto, or a preparation similar, is used to a considerable extent for imparting a yellow color to butter.

CALIFORNIA.

From L. Tomasini, manager of Dairyman's Union of California, San Francisco, Cal.:

The local laws against adulteration are ineffectual, as persons convicted of selling oleomargarin as pure butter were fined but $5, whereas the cost of arrest and conviction to this institution was $200 in each case. We were instrumental in bringing before our last legislature a pure-butter bill which passed both houses, but for some unexplainable reason was pocketed by the governor. This will give you an idea of the extent of the adulterations of foods in this State, and you will readily perceive how helpless we are at present. Local federal authorities instead of taking an interest in these matters seem to show considerable antagonism.

18

From J. H. Hood, M. D., and A. J. Hassler, of Haywards:

Some time ago we noticed an advertisement in a newspaper wherein a certain store offered for sale, among other drugs, a 3-ounce bottle of spirit of camphor for 10 cents. This low price somewhat surprised us, and we therefore bought a bottle with the view of determining where this store made its profit. The 3-ounce bottle turned out to be a 2-ounce short flint glass Blake, and its contents measured 15 fluid drachms. But as even 2 ounces of good spirit of camphor in a flint glass bottle does not allow much, if any, profit if sold at 10 cents, we decided to examine into the equality of this bargain of ours. We found the stuff to be rather less than half the standard strength in camphor, and made with as weak an alcohol as possible. We made an analysis with the following result, as compared with the spirit of camphor of the United States Pharmacopœia:

	Bazar sample.	U. S. P.
Camphor	43	100
Alcohol	553	700
Water	404	200
Total	1.000	1.000

This rather opened our eyes as to the manner in which these stores make their profits, for, as may be plainly seen, the cost of this preparation is very much less than that of a standard article.

The result of this experiment led us to make further purchases of drugs, etc., from various grocery and other similar establishments in San Francisco and Alameda County.

Asafœtida gum.—We bought 1 pound of asafœtida from a retail grocer, and paid 35 cents for it, which was a great deal more than it was worth. The sample is about as poor a lot of asafœtida as we ever saw, and must have been refuse from some lot rejected by druggists, for no reputable druggist would sell such rubbish.

Senna leaves.—With the exception of two lots, all the senna leaves we got were of fair average quality of East India senna, at prices ranging from 2½ cents to 5 cents an ounce. Two samples, sold and labeled as "Alexandrian senna," were moldy and worm-eaten.

Glycerin.—We examined six samples of glycerin and found only one that was of the required specific gravity. In one sample glucose was present to the extent of 21 per cent; the others being only reduced with water, to the average amount of 10 per cent. The price was in each case 10 cents for a 2-ounce bottle.

Seidlitz powders.—Seidlitz powders, as purchased by us at grocery stores, were uniformly of short weight. The heaviest was 40 grains short, and the lightest 48 grains of the seidlitz mixture. The tartaric acid averaged 30 grains, instead of 35 grains. Two lots had Epsom salts and one lot Glauber salts added, to increase the active property.

Ammonia water.—Two samples examined were both of the same strength, containing 7.5 per cent of ammonia, and were sold at 15 cents a pint. Strength thus being sacrificed for an apparently low price.

The most of the other articles bought were of fair average quality, with the exception of tincture of arnica, which in every case was about half the pharmacopœial strength, as compared with a standard tincture prepared by us.

From Mr. Searley, of the California Pharmaceutical Association:

English glucose is almost free of sulphuric acid. Some American glucose is also good, but most of it is contaminated.

COLORADO.

From J. T. Flower, State Dairy Commissioner, Denver, Colo.:

A national law covering the subject would, in my opinion, be beneficial, as it is a notorious fact that nearly every article in that line is more or less adulterated.

From J. W. Goss, president State Dairy Association, Hygiene, Colo.:

We have since July 1, 1893, a law which aims to compel the branding of oleo so it shall be sold for what it is.

A national food and drug law would, in my opinion, be of great benefit to the people.

From G. C. Miller, secretary of the Colorado State Dairy Association, Longmont, Colo.:

At various sessions of the Colorado Dairy Association, the subject of a pure-food bill has been discussed, and a bill passed by Congress on the subject would meet the approval of our association, and also of all other good and law-abiding people.

We also have a beekeepers' association. Straight comb honey will bring 15 cents, while the strained honey sells for only 8 cents. The reason for this, is because a spurious article is sold as pure honey, and beekeepers are compelled to meet this fraud in the market. I trust the pure-food and drug bill will become law in the near future.

From J. H. Wheat, Black Hawk, Colo.:

I know butter to be fraudulent. Oleo is sold here and called creamery butter; maple sugar is also adulterated; California honey is glucose; buckwheat flour is coarse wheat flour (shorts) mixed; some whisky is diluted alcohol colored with burnt sugar. In beer the brewers use laurel leaves, fish berries, and grains of Paradise.

CONNECTICUT.

From C. A. Rapelye, Secretary Board of Pharmacy Commissioners, Hartford, Conn.:

In regard to preventing adulteration of drugs, I am of the opinion that that is largely done by wholesale druggists and drug millers, if at all, and there is not much doubt that it is. I don't believe the retail trade has the facilities or generally the disposition to adulterate drugs, unless it be possibly in the case of laudanum. Laws can not prevent this thing without money and power to execute them, and in this State we have neither placed in our hands. I am of the opinion that United States laws can not be passed that will govern this matter which can be made equitable. The Paddock bill aimed to accomplish something in this line, but it was manifestly unjust and raised the opposition it deserved. The matter must be reached through the manufacturers and large handlers, who have the opportunities, and not through the retailers, who do not have them.

From Dr. George Austin Bowen, master Connecticut State Grange, and president State Dairy Association, Woodstock, Conn.:

I believe that almost every item of our commercial foods is adulterated or contains injurious ingredients, but I have no case now in mind concerning which I could go into court and testify under oath. This has been going on for so long a time that the public have come to believe that adulteration is necessary. It is not only our foods but the medicines and drugs which we depend upon for the restoration to health, when that health has been oftentimes impaired by these adulterated foods. It seems to me that, of all things that should be protected from adulterations and frauds, these remedies to restore us to a normal condition should be the best protected.

Thirty-odd years ago, when I was a student of medicine, we were taught how to detect frauds regarding the various drugs then in use. It was as much a part of our education in materia medica to know the frauds as the true articles, and it seems to me that the frauds have been multiplying since then with a greater power than ever known in bacterial life.

We have no preventive laws of importance in our State that I am acquainted with. We endeavored last winter to get through a pure-food bill. It went through the house all right but got lodged somewhere in the senate. We did, however, get through a splendid oleo bill, based largely upon that in operation in Massachusetts, and taking some of the good points from Ohio. This is now in operation in our State and is having a good effect in obliging oleo to be sold uncolored for what it is.

I can conceive of no more beneficial law than a national food and drug law which would compel a proper branding of all articles of food or drugs that are sold in our markets. It seems to me that these fundamental conditions for the health of the people can not be too closely guarded. Agriculture is said to be the foundation of national prosperity. We do not go to the bottom of it, for food and health are the foundations upon which our whole social structure rests.

Our cities and towns are all beginning to understand the importance of the milk question and are agitating for a proper inspection, but as yet we have nothing of the kind. Our daily milk supply is adulterated in many ways, to the great detriment of infant life, and needs a restraining influence from State authority.

The following is from the Connecticut Agricultural Experiment Station Report for 1887, pages 105, 106:

IMPERIAL GRANUM.

CCLXXIX, as described by the proprietor, "Imperial Granum, the Great Medicinal Food." This justly celebrated dietetic preparation is in composition principally the gluten derived by chemical process from very superior growths of wheat. A solid extract. The invention of an eminent French chemist. It has acquired the reputation of being an incomparable aliment for the growth and protection of infants and children. The salvator for invalids and the aged, etc.

Analysis.

	Imperial Granum.	Wheat flour (average of 25 analyses).
Water	11.10	12.56
Ash	.33	.56
Albuminoids, including gluten	10.13	11.28
Fiber	.10	.27
Nitrogen-free extract	77.58	74.13
Fat	.82	1.20
	100.00	100.00
Cost per pound	$1.00	$0.025-0.05

The Imperial Granum contains 77.24 per cent of wheat starch with possibly some dextrin. The quantity of dextrin and dextrose is not more than 1.8 per cent. The only wide difference between the figures given above for granum and wheat flour is in the cost per pound. The granum can not be distinguished in chemical composition and properties from wheat flour slightly browned, which cooked as a porridge has long been used and prized as a food for infants and invalids.

It does not consist principally of the gluten of wheat, and is in no respect superior as food to good wheat flour.

From W. I. Bartholomew, secretary and treasurer Connecticut Dairymen's Association, Putnam, Conn.:

The matter of the adulteration of foods and drugs has been several times discussed in the meetings of our association and the consensus of the opinions was that such adulterations prevailed to an alarming extent, and that preventive laws were much needed. A bill for this purpose was presented to our last legislature, but for some reason failed to secure passage. But we secured a law, about to take effect, that oleomargarine, if offered for sale, shall not resemble yellow butter. It is stated that in consequence of this but 5 dealers have taken out licenses as against 69 last year, and over 200 in Rhode Island (which is in the same revenue district) this year. I think the brands of foods and drugs should honestly indicate their character.

DISTRICT OF COLUMBIA.

The Washington Star of April 8, 1893, contained the two following articles, which need no comment:

INFANTS AND ADULTERATED MILK.

As shown by Dr. John S. Billings, in his recent lecture before the Sanitary League of the District, the death rate of colored infants under one year of age in this city is 696 out of every 1,000, and of white infants of the same age 273 per 1,000. Right behind this appalling statement comes the almost equally startling statement of the superintendent of dairy products, Chemist J. D. Hird, that "90 per cent of the milk coming into Washington is robbed of part of its cream, and 50 per cent of it is colored."

May not this be the explanation of the enormous death rate of infants during their first year, when milk alone forms their sole article of nourishment? It seems to me that this is a vital question, and demands pretty serious consideration from the District Commissioners, and if not from them then from the Sanitary League.

The chancellor of the Maryland Board of Health reports that 3,673 more infants died during the year 1882 in the city of New York, when there were no milk inspectors, than during 1883, when the milk inspectors were at work confiscating adulterated milk.

The city chemist of New Orleans, in his report to the board of health, shows that New Orleans has been paying $300,000 yearly for the water to adulterate the milk supply of that city.

In addition to the evils of adulteration there are others connected with our milk supply which demand the most careful scrutiny. It has been conclusively proven that milk from a tuberculous cow may contain the bacilli of tuberculosis. From inspection, through the water added to the milk, or even from the water used in cleansing the milk cans, the germs of typhoid fever, diphtheria, scarlet fever, and cholera may be introduced into the human system. It has been demonstrated (see Brit. M. J. for January, 1893) that cows may contract scarlet fever and induce the disease in children through the milk.

M. Miguel, in Chi. J. of the Royal Microscopical Society, says he found in 1 cubic centimeter (about 16 drops) of milk, on its arrival at his laboratory only two hours after being taken from the cow, 9,000 microörganisms. In one hour more the number had increased to 31,750, while in twenty-four hours after leaving the cow the 16 drops contained over 5,000,000 germs.

Prof. Bang, of Copenhagen, observes that bacilli of tuberculosis found in milk, cream, and butter were not destroyed by scalding at a temperature of 150° F. Even 160° did not render milk free from disease-breeding germs.

These facts being undisputed, it would seem that no greater service could be rendered to the people of this city than for the proper authorities to thoroughly investigate this whole question of our milk supply and not trust to the analysis of an occasional pint here and there.

HARRY O. HALL.

APRIL 7, 1893.

DRUGS IN MILK.

Would it not be well for the District authorities while investigating the quality of milk sold in the city to go a step further and inquire as to use of antiseptics therein?

Some years ago I was, as an attorney, thrown in contact with the milk business, as conducted by retailers, and was astounded to find the use of antiseptics as one of the concomitants. One large firm went so far as to advertise "nonsouring milk," and smaller dealers were compelled, in self-defense, to furnish the same quality. To me, who had been reared on a farm, where it is known that milk begins to sour at once upon being taken from the cow, the heresy of "nonsouring milk" was simply horrible.

No matter what drug is used to prevent souring, the partaking of it in such small portions as with children can have but serious results through accumulation in the system, and I trust the health department will interpose their fiat. Watered milk is not injurious if pure water be used; but drugs of any nature should be peremptorily tabooed.

LAWYER.

FLORIDA.

From Prof. Norman J. Robinson, State chemist, Agricultural Department, State of Florida, Tallehassee, Fla.:

Our State has only some general statutes against food and drug adulteration which, I think, are very imperfectly enforced, as there is no special officer whose business it is to investigate the matter or see to the execution of the law.

GEORGIA.

From John M. McCandless, chemist, Atlanta, Ga.:

In my opinion, a law providing for a close and stringent inspection of food and drugs is very necessary all over the country. I believe, however, that to be of any vital force or effect the law should be national in its character so that adulterators in one State can not hide behind the laws or the lack of laws in another State.

From R. J. Redding, director of the Georgia Experiment Station, Experiment, Ga.:

I am of the opinion that a national food and drug law, if properly administered, would conduce to the health of every consumer.

From E. M. Wheat, president of the Georgia Pharmaceutical Association:

You will see from the Georgia pharmaceutical laws that this State has a very good law upon the subject of drug adulteration, and the officers are very vigilant in having those laws carried out; therefore, I hardly think that we have any adulteration in drugs.

So far as I know, there is very little adulteration in food articles in this State. There is a great deal of so-called cider manufactured here that, of course, is adulterated, and I think very injurious.

ILLINOIS.

From Dr. Samuel Kennedy, PH. G., secretary board of health, Shelbyville, Ill.:

As to your question regarding the adulteration of children's foods, dairy and pharmaceutical products, I hardly know how to answer, as it seems to me impossible to draw the line distinguishing between what is and what is not an adulterant. I know of a large number of pharmaceutical products which are made up by our (so-called) pharmacists, but they are not properly prepared. It does not seem, however, that I would be justified in saying they are adultered.

From A. W. Hutchins, secretary board of trade, Elgin, Ill.:

Lard is used to adulterate cheese.

From L. R. Bryant, president Cider and Vinegar Association, Princeton, Ill.:

I do not think spurious cider is manufactured to such a noticeable extent as vinegar is. There is no doubt, however, that in some seasons large quantities are sold in bulk. The so-called champagne cider sold by soda-water vendors does not contain any cider.

The adulteration of vinegar is mainly in two ways: (1) By coloring spirit vinegar to imitate cider vinegar, and (2) by the use of injurious acids in weak vinegar to give it the appearance of greater strength.

The imitating of cider vinegar by coloring spirit vinegar is very largely done, and it not only defrauds the consumer but works great injury to the genuine cider-vinegar maker. I have no doubt that more than four-fifths of the vinegar sold in Illinois as cider, apple, or fruit vinegar is nothing but colored spirit vinegar. As to the extent of the use of injurious acids in vinegar, I am not prepared to say, but think they are used more or less by makers of very cheap vinegar.

State laws regulating the manufacture and sale of vinegar have been passed in a number of States, and where properly framed and enforced have been effective, as in New York and Minnesota.

In this State there is no vinegar law that is of any value. In 1891 an effort was made to pass a law, but it was not successful. I understood the same bill was introduced this winter, but I do not know what prospect there is for its passage.

The efforts to secure national legislation have taken two forms. First, the Paddock pure-food bill was generally advocated by the cider-makers as being in the line desired; second, the repeal or amendment of the vinegar law of 1879, which permits the distilling of a low grade of alcohol for vinegar without payment of any tax, and without Government supervision.

What cider-vinegar makers specially complain of is that the spirit-vinegar men are allowed the exclusive privilege of distilling free alcohol, and then take the liberty of coloring and branding it and selling it on the superior reputation of cider vinegar.

INDIANA.

From George W. Benton, chemist of the health department of Indianapolis, Ind.:

Our city has not as yet considered it important to carry on any systematic study of adulterants. Our board of health, however, feels the importance of it, and we hope in time to establish such investigations.

As to laws relating to foods, etc., we are poor indeed. It is next to impossible to make a case in even a plain matter of adulteration of milk, as the law requires that we not only prove the fact of adulteration, but that the violator knew the article was adulterated, and that it was intentional to defraud, etc. We have won only three cases in a year on that basis, and lost many others on failure to prove the last two clauses.

We have done nothing with cheese, but I have detected the presence of refined lard in some quantity in several cases in the examination of butter.

In the way of milk, at least one dairy company uses or has used a milk preparation which, without ultimate analysis, seemed to be mainly dextrine, or something closely resembling it. Our crusade on milk dealers in the autumn and winter of 1892, although not resulting in many convictions, has resulted in giving us a season almost free from trouble of the kind.

From Mortimer Levering, La Fayette, Ind.:

There are no State laws, no local laws, but laws preventing the sale of bogus foods and drugs would be eminently beneficial to the credulous masses of Western farmers.

From William L. Mollering, pharmacist, Fort Wayne, Ind.:

No butter and cheese adulterants have come under my observation with the exception of butter colors, which are usually prepared from tumeric.

From Dr. J. A. Muret, Madison, Ind.:

I have found it necessary in my practice to recommend a change of milkmen for selling adulterated milk to the people and sick babies.

From Ernst Stahlhuth & Co., druggists and pharmacists, Columbus, Ind.:

I have made no examination of butter recently. Some butter is sold which is a mixture of all grades churned with milk and colored with some proprietary butter color.

Impure baking powders are sold here.

Some time ago I made an examination of cream of tartars and found more specimens of it adulterated than I did pure. I found no adulterated cream of tartar in drug stores, it being the usual kind found in groceries. The adulterants consisted of starch, chalk, alum, plaster of paris, and acid phosphate of lime.

The most of the cayenne peppers sold here by druggists in the powder is mixed with corn meal, as is also the prepared mustard sold by grocers. Adulterated saltpeter is also sold.

IOWA.

From R. W. Crawford, wholesale druggist, Fort Dodge, Iowa:

I am and have been actively engaged in the drug business for twenty-five years, and use care in the drugs I dispense. I find but few adulterations. The worst lot I ever received was from Detroit, Mich., which I returned, the goods being powdered goods—black pepper and others—loaded with terra alba. The capsicum of commerce is said to be very impure, loaded with something, and presumably before it is imported.

KANSAS.

From H. W. McKinney, M. D., health officer, Hutchinson, Kans.:

Our State board of health recommended the enactment of more perfect laws governing the practice of medicine, collection of vital statistics, and other good things, but it seemed our legislature was so busy in fighting for party supremacy that nearly everything that was preeminently needed was ignored or forgotten. I have made some investigations in a general way, and have reason to believe that many, perhaps very many, articles of food are adulterated, notably in the spice line. You can purchase a pound of ground mustard, spice, cloves, or cinnamon, or a pound of cream of tartar from a greengrocer for one-half what a reliable druggist of our city will charge for the same article. I can say for the druggists of our city that you can seldom find on their shelves what is termed commercial drugs (cheap drugs), although they sell black pepsin, as they say their trade demands it. It is my candid opinion that the enactment and rigid enforcement of a national food and drug law, such as you speak of, together with laws by the States governing their own trade, would be productive of much good.

KENTUCKY.

From Dr. Wiley Rogers, PH. D., commissioner of public charities, Louisville, Ky.:

I have not made any special investigation relative to food and drug adulterations for several years. I was then sanitary inspector for the city. I am now a commissioner of public charities, and we have pure food and drugs for our city hospital, which I visit once a week, for there I examine the food that is given to the sick. I know that food adulteration is largely on the increase, and all that is necessary to prove it will be a thorough investigation. As to drugs, in which I am most interested, my opinion is that you can get pure drugs if you pay for them. I have been in the drug business since 1858.

From E. Y. Johnson, pharmacist, Louisville, Ky.:

The only experience I have had in food and drug adulterations was in making an analysis of several samples of cream tartar, about two years ago. I tested samples from four or five groceries, and found in one sample as much as 75 per cent sulph. calcium. In the others I found calc. sulph. as well as tartrate calcium, instead of the bi. tart. pot. My reason for conducting the tests was to ascertain why the groceries could retail cream tartar for about what I paid wholesale.

LOUISIANA.

From Erich Brand, 847 Magazine street, New Orleans, La.:

The only adulterant I have ever seen used in milk was water, and lately I have seen some specimens of cream cheese adulterated with some amylaceous substance, most likely corn starch.

From R. N. Girling, New Orleans, La.:

The board of health of this city, of which Dr. L. F. Salomon is secretary and Dr. A. L. Metz is chemist, has for several years been actively engaged in preventing the adulteration of milk by vigorously prosecuting the dealers. The only form of adulteration has, I believe, been the addition of water. A great improvement has been effected in the sanitation of the cow stables and in the quality of the water supplied to the animals.

From Dr. R. J. Mainegra, 84 Washington avenue, New Orleans, La.:

I am perfectly satisfied that a great deal of butter is consumed in this city which contains large proportions of beef tallow and cotton-seed oil, with coloring matter.

MAINE.

From W. H. Jordan, director agricultural experiment station, Maine State College, Orono, Me.:

The only adulterant I personally know to be used in this State in dairy products is boric acid or the so-called preservaline, which is used by those who are sending cream out of the State, as a means of preventing fermentation.

MARYLAND.

From Dr. James A. Stuart, secretary of the State Board of Health:

The amount of information the State Board of Health is able to give in regard to the adulteration of food and drugs is very meager, owing to the very limited appropriation made by the State legislature for this purpose. Since my appointment in April I have employed two inspectors, one for marine and the other for animal foods. The general results of such food inspections as we have been able to prosecute have been remarkably good for such limited opportunities. There are local laws, both State and municipal, but too vague and without support of inspectors.

A national food and drug law would be of great use and benefit to this as well as all other communities in this country.

From Dr. Tonry in the Baltimore Sun:

If you really want a fruit jelly which is made wholly and entirely from raspberries, strawberries, or currants do not expect to find it commercially, but procure the fruit and make it for yourself. The best commercial jelly imitations are made from good apples to which is added glucose, sugar to sweeten, tartaric acid to give tartness, and the composition is transformed into fruit jelly by the addition of the sirups after which it is named.

A common article is made from the cores and parings of apples and the addition of glucose, tartaric acid, aniline colors, and a little salicylic acid, and the compound is converted into a fruit jelly with the addition of a little of the fruit sirup to help the illusion. The cost of this article by the bucket will not be over 4 or 5 cents a pound, while the better quality will cost 12 to 15 cents. In this line of goods, when you purchase in the market or at the grocery store an article to which the maker is ashamed to attach his name, you may expect to find, as I did in an article purchased in one of our markets, very much glucose, no sugar, aniline enough to give color, and no raspberry sirup. The article cost 15 cents a pound and had on the package a printed label with the words, "Raspberry jelly." Only that and nothing more; but the vendor assured me that the article was really a pure raspberry jelly, and as I find it not always advisable to appear to know too much I did not express my doubt of the manifestly false assertion. Personally, I do not object to pure apple butter with a little pure glucose and some raspberry sirup, sugar, and tartaric acid. It would be easier and better to adopt a name which would give a more correct idea of the compound, but I think I would draw the line, between good and suspicious articles of this class, at apple skins and apple cores, second or third grade glucose, and aniline colors.

From Dr. E. T. Duke, secretary of board of health, Cumberland, Md.:

There are some adulterations in certain essences, laudanums, paregoric, etc., sold in the country stores. These goods are purchased in large cities. The adulterants are not injurious to health, I think.

From Columbus V. Emich, druggist, Baltimore, Md.:

I am unable to give you any reliable statement as to adulterations of food, drugs, etc. That it prevails to a very great extent is, I think, clearly the case, and the evidence of that to my mind is the advertised rates at which many goods are offered and sold. As men do not work for work's sake and glory, it is reasonable to suppose that goods offered far below rates at which goods can be bought at first hand, are prepared for the special rates at which they are offered. This, however, is not the information you wish, but the general condition is all that I am aware of so far as direct evidence will go.

Dr. Chancellor, secretary of the Maryland State Board of Health, in an address before the convention of the National Food and Dairy Commissioners of 1892, held in Washington, D. C., March 30 and 31, 1892, said ·

Now, sir, in accordance with a suggestion or resolution—I do not remember which—that was introduced here yesterday that each member of this association should, as far as possible, see a member or members of the delegation from his State, and urge the passage of this bill, I happened yesterday afternoon to meet with a prominent member of the Maryland delegation on my way home, and I took occasion to bring this matter to his attention, and he said he was entirely in accord with the object of the bill, but he doubted very much the constitutionality of it, and his doubts were based upon its possible interference with State's rights. I told him thirty years or more ago I thought as he did, but the logic of events had convinced me that the proper thing to do now was to keep the States right, and above all things to keep these people right who were poisoning our people and our children, and who will continue to poison our children and our children's children unless some action is taken by the National Government.

I am very well satisfied, sir, notwithstanding the success which Massachusetts and New Jersey have had in this matter, that all States that will follow the course which they have pursued will have great difficulty indeed in getting to the point they have reached, and if we can reach that point by one single bound I think it would be much better, and the only way to do it is through national laws.

MASSACHUSETTS.

Although this State has probably the best executed laws upon adulteration, owing to the liberal appropriations made and the efficient direction given the service, while some reduction has been made in sophisticated selling, still the work goes on. The report of the board of health for February, 1893, shows that out of 275 samples analyzed 107 varied from the legal standard, the per cent of adulteration being 38.9 of the goods examined.

The milk examined showed 66 per cent adulterated.

Samples of honey bearing the following label were found to contain 10 per cent of glucose: On one side "Pure Honey," on the opposite side "Extracted Honey, Geo. D. Powell, 81 Third street, Brooklyn, N. Y."

The samples of drugs found to be adulterated were red wine and washed sulphur.

A sample of baking powder examined by Dr. Harrington, chemist of the Massachusetts Board of Health, "was chiefly coarse hominy."

From the Massachusetts Dairy Commission:

In relation to laws relating to milk, we have a high standard, viz, 13 per cent solids, with very severe penalties for adulteration. For the purpose of enforcing that law, any milk having less than 13 per cent solids is deemed to be adulterated.

Our State is well provided with laws regulating the sale of imitation butter, with the intent that the sale shall be confined to an honest sale of the goods, if such a thing is possible, though as a matter of fact there is something peculiar about oleomargarin, in so far as it seems to benumb the moral sensibilities of those who have the handling of it, and although there is unquestionably an oleo which may, under some circumstances, be of benefit to the public, the sale of the ordinary commercial article is very closely and intimately connected with fraud and deceit.

Among the various restrictive measures on this subject, the most important is a law which absolutely prohibits the sale of any imitation of yellow butter. This law has been before our State supreme court once and been pronounced constitutional.

A writ of error has taken this decision to the United States Supreme Court, where it is now pending. Meanwhile another case has gone to the State supreme court, raising additional points; so that this law is now practically of no effect and will not be until the supreme court sustains it. The laws relative to marks on tubs, marks on wrappers, giving notice by restaurant keepers, etc., are fairly well enforced and have done much to prevent the irregular sales of oleomargarin. In fact, the most of it that is sold in this State at present is sold by agents for the large wholesalers, who sell only by the tub and then only on orders, so that most of the goods so sold are purchased knowingly by the consumer, and there is no element of deceit in the transaction so far as I am at present advised.

So far as dairy products are concerned, I do not see what effect a national law could have in promoting the efficiency of our laws, but there would be great gain if the laws of the different States could be similar. In the matter of oleomargarin, which, in a State like Massachusetts, is received entirely from other States, there being no manufactory here, national legislation might possibly be of some assistance.

From Eben M. Holbrook, refiner of champagne cider for bottling, South Sherborn, Mass.:

By the unanimous vote of the Fruit-Growers', Cider and Cider-Vinegar Makers' Association of Massachusetts, a request was made of the Senators and Representatives in Congress from this State to render such assistance as they could towards the enactment of the Paddock pure-food bill at the time it was before Congress.

MICHIGAN.

From J. S. Foster, manager Genesee Fruit Company, Lansing Mills, Lansing, Mich.:

We are heartily in favor of a national food and drug law that will compel all manufacturers to brand their products by their true names. While we have no evidence that would be worth anything to you, we do know that there is scarcely an article of food offered by the grocers throughout the country that is not adulterated.

Cider is adulterated to a less degree, perhaps, than almost any other drink or food product you might mention. It consists mostly in compositions of water and sugar with apple extract colored to look like cider. It is not very injurious but is a fraud and injures the honest manufacturer. Genuine cider is sometimes charged to such a degree with salicylic acid to hold it sweet, as to make it, in our opinion, injurious to health. As to vinegar, we used to find sulphuric acid quite frequently, but the chief adulteration of vinegar at present is water. Some manufacturers get it down so fine as to get it about three times as much water as vinegar. We have just tested a sample of vinegar sold for 40 grains strength and for pure apple-cider vinegar that showed but 19 grains acidity and not a particle of cider about it. Grocers have no means of testing it except by taste and they are defrauded in about 90 per cent of the vinegar they buy. Corn vinegar is colored with burnt sugar and sold in about 90 per cent of cases for cider vinegar.

We would be very much pleased to see a law passed that would shut out such shams. It would be a good thing for the consumer and for the dealer and manufacturer of honest goods.

MINNESOTA.

From Noyes Bros. & Cutler, St. Paul, Minn.:

We do not think children's prepared foods are adulterated. We do not think pharmaceutical preparations of respectable houses are adulterated. Essential oils are adulterated. Substitutes are common. Medicinal powders are not always the best. Just where adulteration begins and ends, it is hard to say. A ground mustard not perfectly pure is adulterated but is as good for many purposes and for some purposes better than the full strength mustard.

From Berndt Anderson, dairy and food commissioner, St. Paul, Minn.:

The butter made in this State is a pure article without adulteration of any kind. The only fraud we have to contend with is oleomargarin, and that is not made in this State, but shipped in from Chicago. We are in hopes that the time will come when we can eliminate that vile compound. The State Dairy and Food Department of this State has the enforcement of all laws of this character.

MISSOURI.

From Theodore Ilg, chemist, St. Louis, Mo.:

As to results and effect of our preventive laws, so far as dairy products are concerned, in which the law has been very strictly enforced, the object of the law has been reached very successfully, and with less trouble than anticipated. In consequence we now have in St. Louis a very satisfactory grade of dairy products. We do have local laws here concerning all sorts of adulterations. The dairy-product law, however, is the only one enforced and for which an office has been created.

The benefits of a national food and drug law are numerous and obvious, and in my opinion such laws are a necessity and a protection the public should have. It not only puts a premium on honesty, but also protects the people's health and life. Such laws would also be very instructive to the ignorant class, who before never thought of the quality of their food stuffs and would soon teach them how to select wholesome food.

From Charles C. Bell, Cider and Cider-Vinegar Makers' Association, Boonville, Mo.:

It is my opinion that the adulteration of food is much greater than most people have any idea. This is especially true of vinegar.

By request of the above association, I drafted a bill in 1891 and sent it to the Missouri legislature, which was passed, but it is not enforced to any extent, like a good many other laws we have on our statute books. The chief provision in said law is to compel the manufacturer to brand his output, true to name; in other words to stop the branding of spurious vinegar as cider, or apple vinegar.

In my opinion national legislation on this subject is very necessary, but I fear that our law-makers in Congress assembled will not think it worth while to consider the subject. They have too much politics on hand to consider any pure-food measure.

From Capt. Henry G. Sharp, commissary U. S. Army, St. Louis, Mo.

The information I have gathered of food adulteration has been the result of the work of others, as I have not had time to make any extended investigation. I am deeply interested in the subject, and know of no other which is more important.

While some of the State laws are quite comprehensive, the fact is, none are the same or are enforced with the same honesty of purpose in the different States. Therefore we should have a national law on the subject, and this law should be most sweeping. It should be an offense for a manufacturer of food products to have on his premises any article used as an adulterant. • The opponents of such a measure have declared such a law unconstitutional, but they are not yet members of the Supreme Court, the authority from which we learn of the validity of the laws of Congress. Neither the Executive nor the Supreme Court announce the action they will take on a bill submitted for approval, or an act of Congress, the constitutionality of which has been questioned, before it reaches them.

From Albert J. Funch, druggist, Eighth and Soulard streets, St. Louis, Mo.:

Adulterations of food and drugs are carried on now on an enormous scale. It is no longer a secret. For example, take vanilla bean, opium, and many other important drugs. I have bought vanilla from different drug houses and have often been obliged to return the same, owing to its inferior quality. Opium of a pure quality is especially hard to get. The producers often exhaust the pure gum with alcohol, making a strong tincture, which is sold on the market, and then triturate the bulk of the opium with poppy leaves and put it on the market as first-class gum opium, which the jobbers sell as such, yet purchased by them as second-class. Vanilla is treated in the same way.

As individual dealers we can not make the necessary investigations, owing to the expense.

Food adulterations are plentiful; impure cheese, butter, preserves, baking powders, ice cream, vinegar, and many other articles are passed upon the consumer as pure. I have investigated some cheese from my grocer and found it so ingeniously adulterated as to deceive the ordinary buyer.

From Otto A. Hartwig, M. D., St. Louis, Mo.:

All powdered drugs are more or less adulterated with inert substances, such as flaxseed meal, fine sawdust, etc., unless obtained from some reliable dealer, regardless of cost. Concerning children's food I am of the opinion that the patent and proprietary articles sold as such are mostly vile compositions of starch, sugar, malt, and gums, and at best they are old and stale when procured by the customer. Frequently they are full of vermin, as any druggist can tell, and often by his own experience, when the customer returns them. I have seen some of them actually alive with insects and worms when the stuff had been freshly procured from the wholesale house.

From Mr. John Whittaker, a large packer in St. Louis, Mo.:

I am credibly informed that some, if not a great deal, of the so-called "refined" lard of commerce does not contain a particle of lard and is made entirely from cotton-seed oil and acid-bleached or washed tallow. It is when cool almost odorless, but I presume when put in the pan and warmed it would more nearly indicate its character. If these statements to me are true, I think it is a shame that they should use the word "lard" at all.

From Hon. W. S. Cowherd, mayor, Kansas City, Mo.:

As to butter adulterants, I have discovered nothing which has not been already published in the bulletin of the Division of Chemistry of the Department of Agriculture. These adulterations consist chiefly of coloring matters (such as turmeric) and foreign fats. The law taxing oleomargarin, butterin, etc., has resulted in causing all large manufacturers to label their products and has largely diminished the sale of artificial butter under the name of the genuine article.

A good deal of the "creamery" butter sold here, however, is what is known as "renovated," i. e., made from old, inferior, and rancid products which are washed to rid them of the free butyric acid and colored uniformly with turmeric, and treated with boric acid and like antizymotic chemicals, and put on the market as creamery butter.

The most common form of adulteration of milk practiced here, as elsewhere, is the removal of cream or the addition of water, or both. Formerly, I have found cane sugar (added to increase the specific gravity) and sodium bicarbonate (to produce froth and neutralize acidity), together with annotto, as coloring matter. I have also found in samples starch and boric acid, and in a few cases salicylic acid. These latter forms of adulterations are becoming rare in this city, owing to the very heavy penalty.

The infants' foods sold here are all proprietary articles, sold in closed packages, and, however their physiological effects may differ from those claimed for them, they could not under our city laws be deemed adulterated.

As to pharmaceutical preparations, although hardly in the line of my work, a number of these have been examined, chiefly for use of the committee on adulteration of the Missouri State Pharmaceutical Association.

The result of these will be found in the annual report of that society for 1892.

Any further information I am able to give will be gladly furnished you at any time, especially for use of the Division of Chemistry in the Department of Agriculture, to which the chemists all over the country are so much indebted for information on recent methods of adulteration and the most approved means of detecting the same.

From William H. Avis, president Clarksville Cider and Vinegar Company, St. Louis, Mo.:

Our knowledge of the adulteration of food in this community is confined to vinegar. In 1891 a law was passed by the legislature of Missouri, and, while penalties were attached, there was no enforcement clause. The law is therefore a dead letter for want of enforcement. This law was compiled in the interest of the horticultural society of Missouri, and while the apple-vinegar men were consulted, the fear that even this law could not be passed prevented the framers from making it more operative. It was a groundless fear, and if the law had been perfected it doubtless would have passed both branches of our legislature.

There are so few engaged in the manufacture of pure apple vinegar in this State that any further legislation would become a burden in a pecuniary sense upon them, and we have concluded to wait in hopes that Congress will come to our relief by a passage of a law similar to the Paddock pure food-bill.

The sentiment of the community on this score is largely in favor of the Government taking the matter in hand. It is almost impossible to pass State or municipal laws of this nature, unless protected by a Government law that would control interstate communication. Should a Government law be enacted we could influence legislation to correspond, and without doubt could have the same passed by our legislature.

MONTANA.

From Dr. J. W. Gunn, health office, Butte, Mont.:

The only methods of adulteration with which I am acquainted are selling oleomargarin for butter and attempts to sell diluted milk at times. There are no food or drug inspectors in this State.

NEBRASKA.

From A. Lamoureux, Rushville, Nebr.:

Milk is adulterated in Rushville by the addition of certain drugs and chemicals which increase the quantity of milk 100 per cent.

NEW HAMPSHIRE.

From Herbert S. Clough, sanitary inspector, board of health, Manchester, N. H.

A large amount of butterin is being sold here through agents who are not punishable under our statutes. It is shipped from Lowell, Mass., here and delivered c. o. d. by a common carrier.

A large part of the milk supply of the city is adulterated. Water is the principal adulterant. Salt and sugar are used to cover the taste and a preparation of annotto to color butterin. Old milk men tell me that 6 quarts of milk are quite often extended into 8.

From N. C. Twombly, M. D., Center Strafford, N. H.

Almost all the whisky and some drugs are adulterated. For instance, I purchased 1 gallon of alcohol for 95 per cent and it was only 55 per cent on testing when I got home.

Some of our flour is adulterated more or less, with a certain kind of earth that comes from the South.*

NEW JERSEY.

From Prof. August Drescher, chemist of the State Board of Health, Newark, N. J.:

I have examined five samples of butter since last summer, three of which were genuine, two of cotton-oil composition.

The general condition of milk in our city for the past year has been, in my experience, good, most of the samples examined by me showing over 12.5 per cent total solids, many of them even over 13 per cent. This excludes a number of samples which were undoubtedly adulterated, i. e., either watered or skimmed, or both.

It has occurred twice in my recent experience that the surfaces of cheese packed in tin foil contained notable quantities of lead, which I consider dangerous, these parts of the cheeses being generally eaten, as well as the inner portions, into which the invasion of the lead has not extended. Both these samples were Limburger cheese. Out of a number of Limburger cheese samples I also discovered one which gave the "murexide reaction," indicative of the employment of urine for "ripening" the cheese. I had heard of this dirty practice, but not believing the story made tests of some samples to get evidence or prove the popular belief to be unfounded.

Children's nursing nipples and fittings, tubings, etc., of India rubber of our market are mostly weighted with minerals. Thus I have found the white India rubber articles loaded with zinc oxide, which forms poisonous salts not intended for infants' stomachs.

Dried apples have come to my attention which contain zinc; one sample also copper.

Laudanum, especially that sold by grocers (unlawfully, only registered pharmacists in our State having the privilege to sell such poisonous drugs), of our market is, in most cases, deficient in morphine strength. I have also found the essence of peppermint, essence of ginger, vanilla, Hoffman's anodyne, especially the articles put up for grocers' use, to be of very inferior quality. One sample of mustard powder, sold at 15 cents per pound, proved to be a mixture containing chromate of lead, chalk (or whiting), Spanish pepper, and Indian meal, together with some real mustard.

Seidlitz powders of deficient weight are, in spite of all legislation, openly sold at the present day.

NEW YORK.

From A. M. Hodge, druggist, Canajoharie, N. Y.:

A little coloring matter prepared from annotto is used somewhat early in the season to give butter a golden tinge, but no other adulterations are practiced that I know of.

The New York City Health Report for 1891, p. 183, states:

The total number of slaughtered animals in New York City for 1891 was 3,107,939, which weighed 533,660,595 pounds. This immense amount of food consisted only of cattle, hogs, sheep and lambs and calves. In addition the amount of live and dressed poultry, dressed beef, sheep, hogs, and calves amounted to 483,624,900 pounds. Over 300,000 pounds more of meat were seized by the inspectors in 1891 than in 1890, including 60,000 pounds more of "bob" veal.

* This is doubtless a mistake.—H. W. W.

From Jesse Owen, 410 West Church street, Elmira, N. Y.:

I have no information that would be new to you, but am sure that some very stringent laws should be made and then enforced against the adulteration of food. I have been quite conversant with the dairy commissioner of New York State. The old commissioner was an active, honest man and did much to keep out oleo.

A man at the icing station in Waverly, N. Y., told my son that they were icing some ten cars a day loaded with Elgin butter made in Chicago and destined for New York City. This butter was packed in tierces. I presume it was oleo.

From Schoellkopf, Hartford & Maclagan, New York:

With regard to the adulteration of food and drugs we beg to say that we only handle imported drugs, and of course the appraisers are here to reject inferior quality, but as a matter of fact they often pass very inferior drugs. We have known of very inferior jalap being allowed through the custom-house. But they go to the other extreme with regard to ipecac, and refuse to admit the root that comes from Carthagena, although, as far as we know, it is fully equal to the Brazilian root.

From Fairchild Bros. & Foster, New York:

Concerning the adulterations of children's foods we would say that we have never heard of such a thing. There are so-called "infants' foods" of very great variety of composition. Some of these are practically baked flour; others malted flour or Liebig's foods; others are simply condensed milk or milk condensed with farinaceous substances or with malted flour; others of dried milk, or milk dried with farinaceous and saccharine matter. We do not see how any of these foods can be considered in any way adulterated foods. If there was a certain definite standard of composition for each variety of infant food then there would be some point of view from which the quality of an infant food could be considered. For instance, if a Liebig food contained glucose not due to the malting of flour it would be considered adulterated, but there is no such adulterated food in existence. If a food stated to be Liebig's food contained anything more than a trace of starch it must be considered to be badly made, but scarcely to be adulterated. It would simply be an imperfect Liebig food. Infants' foods are in the main just what they are represented to be, in so far as their composition is concerned, and every variety of them is employed for the food of infants. There is no such thing as an adulterated infant food to our knowledge.

As to the adulterations of pharmaceutical preparations we can not give you any data. We do not believe that there are any such which would properly be considered adulterated. We believe that in general they conform closely to the statements made concerning their composition and quality; that they will differ mainly owing to the skill and knowledge with which they are prepared, and will not be found to be adulterated in any sense in which that term can be used. Of the dairy products we have no special knowledge.

From W. T. Pettengill, manager Genesee Fruit Company, 501 West street, Holley, N. Y.:

We have a State law governing the sale of vinegar in the State, which has materially improved the quality of all vinegar, but for want of a general law we are handicapped by the "original package" from other States.

The State dairy commissioner has the enforcement of the vinegar law in this State, which he does through subordinates.

I believe a general law governing the branding of all articles of food and drugs would be beneficial in protecting honest manufacturing, and in telling to the buyer what he is getting, and driving from the market articles which would never be used if the consumer knew what they contained.

NORTH CAROLINA.

From H. B. Battle, director North Carolina Agricultural Experiment Station, Raleigh, N. C.:

We have no laws in this State in reference to the adulteration of food and drugs. A proper national law wisely enforced would unquestionably benefit the people of the United States.

NORTH DAKOTA.

From W. S. Parker, secretary of the North Dakota State Board of Pharmacy, Lisbon, N. Dak.:

We have a food and drug adulteration law in this State, and I do not think that it is violated to any great extent. I think that a national food and drug law, compelling the proper branding of all articles of food and drugs shipped from one State to another, would do much more to stop adulterations than could be accomplished in any other way.

OHIO.

From Charles T. P. Fennel, chairman of the American Pharmaceutical Association, Cincinnati, Ohio:

Regarding the laws I am satisfied that they do not accomplish the object desired, viz, the protection of the public in the purchase of all products necessary for subsistence. Legislators do not usually take into consideration social and economic conditions. They fail to discriminate between adulteration in its various differentiations, or to give the proper support for the enforcement of the law, and they offer in the majority of cases, by ambiguous phraseology, opportunities for violations. In fact State laws are absolutely valueless. Nothing can be accomplished until the U. S. Government takes charge of the matter. The framing of a law governing food products should not be a very difficult task. For drugs the United States pharmacopœia should be made the legal authority, with such modifications of maximum and minimum strength to allow for variations.

Frank Kienzle, esq., Columbus, Ohio, sends the two following extracts, but fails to give the name of the paper from which they were clipped, but gives their date as May 2.

UNWHOLESOME ARTICLES.

State Dairy and Food Commissioner McNeal to-day received the reports of analysis made by John H. Westerhoff and Louis Schmidt, including a number of articles of food which had been submitted to them by the deputy commissioners. Among these were 3 samples of maple sirup, one of which, produced by Williams Bros., Detroit, and sold in Cincinnati, is reported to have contained 60 per cent of glucose; another produced by A. E. Idett, Cincinnati, is marked as being a mixture of molasses and glucose, and the third, from the Woodstock Maple Sirup Company, St. Louis, is put down as containing 30 to 35 per cent of glucose.

The most glaring of the adulterations in the list is a sample of coffee, which the chemist says, "was found to consist of pure barley, malted, roasted, and ground. Contains no coffee whatever."

A sample of sweet oil, sold by Eckler & Co., Pleasant Ridge, Ohio, the producer being unknown, is reported to be adulterated with 20 per cent of cotton-seed oil.

Food and Dairy Commissioner McNeal has received from the chemists a number of analyses made of articles of food submitted by his department. Several samples of maple sirup were found to be pure, while a couple of samples of lard were slightly adulterated with stearin. A sample of olive oil, labeled "Huile d'olive vierge," secured from a dealer in Warren, Trumbull County, and handled by a wholesaler in Cleveland, was found to be composed entirely of cotton-seed oil. A glass of currant jelly, made by McMehen, in Wheeling, W. Va., is composed chiefly of apple pulp. Another sample of Chandler's vinegar, sold for malt vinegar, is found to be a distilled article and colored with caramel.

Dr. W. S. West, New Matamoras, Ohio, sends the following:

IMPURE FOOD.

The analyses of a number of food samples by the State dairy and food commissioner, secured from Cincinnati dealers, were made public to-day. Louis Schmidt is the chemist. They are as follows: Maple sirup, from T. J. Wenstrath, 60 per cent glucose; olive oil, A. B. Barnes & Co., pure; maple sirup, Portwood, mixture of molasses and glucose; butter, H. Sicking, artificially colored; maple sirup, Henry Schultz, 30 per cent glucose; apple vinegar, Ehler & Morris, apple and white-wine vinegar and water: white-wine vinegar, Ehler & Morris, pure; maple sirup, D. Telan, pure; sweet oil, W. H. Eckler & Co., 20 per cent cotton-seed oil; apple vinegar, J. J. Jackson, not pure.

From A. Hauenstein, druggist, Bluffton, Ohio:

Drugs from wholesale houses are often adulterated, especially ground goods. I hope something can be done to remedy the evil. I have some now ready to return to them.

From Tim Leroux, president of the Ohio State Cider and Vinegar Makers' Association, Toledo, Ohio:

The cider and vinegar makers and makers of pure fruit products demand a national food law by all means, as we think it is the only law that would prevent the adulteration of food. We have a food law in Ohio, and we have a food commissioner in our State by the name of Dr. F. H. McNeal, with office in Ohio State Building, Columbus, Ohio. We believe the Ohio State food commissioner is doing his very best to keep adulterated food out of the State, but he can not do it successfully. I am personally engaged in the cider-vinegar business, and traveling on the road I find colored spirit vinegar sold in almost every town. This vinegar is made and sold by parties living in other States. In some cases it is branded "pure cider vinegar," but does not contain a particle of cider, hence you can clearly see the necessity of a national food and drug law compelling the branding of all articles of food and drugs, by whom manufactured, and residence of the manufacturer, to enable the Department to find the guilty party.

A special dispatch from Columbus, Ohio, to the Cleveland Leader and Herald of February 22, 1890, is as follows:

ADULTERATED BEER.

Prof. Herman A. Weber, State chemist, at the instance of F. A. Derthick, State food and dairy commissioner, has made a chemical analysis of "Kaiser" beer, manufactured at Bremen, Germany, and imported to this country, where it is sold to those who are able to purchase a costly stimulant or tonic. It is taken for dyspepsia, etc. Prof. Weber discovered that this beer is highly charged with salicylic acid, originally extracted from oil of wintergreen, but now made from coal tar. The acid is an antiseptic. It is frequently used to preserve food and naturally preserves the food in the stomach. Prof. Weber also analyzed Leopold Hoff's Malt Extract, a tonic manufactured in Hamburg, Germany. It also contained large quantities of salicylic acid. * * * Dr. Ashmun, of Cleveland, a member of the State Board of Health, says that salicylic acid is given sometimes for a few days, but it must be discontinued, and as invalids and their physicians should know what is being administered as a tonic, Commissioner Derthick desires to inform them and the public. * * * The developments made by these investigations are to be laid before the legislature in support of the adulterated food bill, which has passed one branch.

From Dr. B. F. McNeal, Ohio dairy and food commission, Columbus, Ohio:

A summary of the analyses of samples taken by the Ohio dairy and food commission during the year ending May, 1893, shows about 64 per cent of the samples analyzed to have been adulterated. The samples were taken from goods found on sale in the open market by men who were not experts in judging the quality of the goods they inspected. The character of the adulterants has been mainly of the class termed noninjurious. Though many substances are used as adulterants which may not be injurious to the healthy stomach, yet when given to the people promiscuously, both healthy and unhealthy, many of them must be injurious in some cases.

The result of the pure-food legislation in the State of Ohio has been effective in reducing and preventing adulteration of foods and drugs in proportion to the active measures taken by our dairy and food commission to execute the law. The laws on our statute books have been and always will be a dead letter unless an active, energetic policy is maintained upon the part of those who are officially charged with their execution.

OREGON.

In a recent paper on the subject of milk and butter, the Hon. W. W. Baker, food commissioner for Oregon, says:

To me this part of my subject is more interesting, because, even with the limited amount of money at my command, I have been enabled to enforce the law in a profitable degree at least.

A considerable amount of imitation butter has been sold in this market during the present winter by wholesalers, who do so by virtue of a Federal license. I have made several arrests and secured as many convictions. Without comment as to the quality of imitation butter, I will quote what Prof. Henry F. Nachtriet, of the Minnesota State University, says, after making many tests:

"The best and cleanest looking samples had a butter odor and taste, and would readily pass for butter. It had a very small variety of living organisms, but a great many spores, which, under favorable conditions, I have no doubt, would germinate. It also contained masses of dead mold, bits of cellulous wood, various colored particles, shreds of hair, bristles, etc. The other 2 samples teemed with life, and yielded microscopic preparations of the mold and bacteria that would have gladdened the heart of the student of biology. The microscope revealed the fact that the greatest variety of life existed in the inner portions of these samples, and that the outer portions contained the greatest quantity of active bacteria. The animals found in the butterine belong to the type of protozoa. Doubtful portions of worms were also noticed. Many of the protozoa, under favorable conditions, pass into a encysted stage or develop spores within protected capsules, and in these conditions lie dormant till the environment is again favorable, and it can hardly be doubted that some of the many spores found in butterine were merely in a dormant state. The great number and variety of organisms found in the samples indicate the use of foul water and a criminally filthy process in making it. There can not be the slightest doubt that the person who eats so promiscuous and lively a mixture as the butterin examined is running great risk, morally as well as physically. The peace and happiness of future generations are greatly involved in the life of the present generation. By indulging in our homes in articles of food filled with spores and seeds of the various classes of the lower organisms we are increasing the dangers of parasitism. Spores that are now harmless may, by gradual adaptation, through more or less circuitous routes, become inimical to the health and happiness of countless millions."

In a letter to Hon. W. S. Mason, mayor of Portland, Oreg., Hon. W. W. Baker says:

In February, 1891, when I assumed the duties of Oregon State food commissioner, I found that my predecessor had not required retailers, hotels, and restaurants to comply with our law regarding dairy products, and as a consequence our markets were full of oleomargarin. In addition to this, I found that no special requirements had been demanded of milk supply dairymen, and as a consequence a very large proportion of the milk and cream was adulterated. A vigorous enforcement of our law soon knocked out the oleomargarin and to a very great extent brought to consumers a good quality of milk. My report shows that there were but two wholesale oleomargarin licenses and no retail license taken out to sell the "stuff" in this State during my two years' term, and, indeed, most of that which had been licensed was still in the wholesalers' hands when my term expired. But during the succeeding thirty days the whole stock was "dumped," and home butter declined from 7½ to 15 cents per pound. No effort has been made to discover whether or not there was any adulterated cheese. My report also shows that a constant vigilance was required to force a supply of good, pure, normal milk.

That there is much adulterated food in our market there is no question—I figure that at least 15 per cent of all foods—but as to how much of it is adulterated with injurious ingredients I have no means of knowing, for the reason that I had no funds at my command to make satisfactory investigations.

PENNSYLVANIA.

From Alonzo Robbins, president of the Pennsylvania Pharmaceutical Examining Board, Eleventh and Vine streets, Philadelphia, Pa.:

You may remember that some time ago I handed to you a copy of last year's proceedings of the Pennsylvania Pharmaceutical Association, in which are recorded my own efforts to enforce the present State law against adulterations. The results are not such as to encourage me to hope for substantial success until the various State laws are supported by a vigorous national law.

From J. A. Miller, secretary of the Pennsylvania Pharmaceutical Association, Harrisburg, Pa.:

The pharmaceutical examining board is required to prosecute all cases of adulteration of drugs and medicines. So far the only cases prosecuted have been for the adulteration of laudanum.

Extract from report of committee on adulterations and deterioration, fifteenth annual meeting of the Pennsylvania Pharmaceutical Association (pp. 39, 40):

It was not considered of any profit to gather drugs and preparations from different stores and have them analyzed, as this work has been so fully done by Prof. Trimble and the students working under him, that we all fully recognize that there is quite a want of conformity to the U. S. Pharmacopœia, which in some cases amounts to more than neglect, indeed must be called a crime.

Neither was it considered advisable to collect specimens for analysis with a view to prosecution, as this work has been so well done by the previous committee that it was decided that the best thing to do was to assist the board of pharmacy in pushing to a conclusion the suits to be instituted on the evidence already in hand. The expenses of the committee, amounting to $45, were caused by the necessity for compensating the principal witnesses for the prosecution for the time lost owing to the law's delay; vouchers for the same have been forwarded to the treasurer. It may be asked what has been obtained in return for the money expended and the work performed. We think that, in the first place, it has given notice to the druggists of the State what they may expect if they violate the law, and has rendered them unable to plead ignorance of the same. In the second place, it has caused an improvement in the strength of the preparations sold, in at least some of the stores of the Commonwealth.

From R. A. Wallis, 3124 Westmont street, Philadelphia, Pa.:

It was my experience while chairman of the committee on adulterations and deteriorations for the Pennsylvania Pharmaceutical Association that, under existing law in this State, prosecutions are useless. It is a dead letter here.

From F. C. Clemson, Reading, Pa.:

To my mind, so long as the consuming public demand cheapness in preference to purity so long will adulterants be made and used.

From William O. Farley, druggist, Lancaster, Pa.:

The only foreign substance incorporated with butter, to my knowledge, is butter color, which is used only in winter to give a golden tinge to what would be otherwise white butter. Butter colors are usually made of annetto or turmeric, held in suspension in cotton-seed or olive oil.

From J. A. Miller, secretary Pharmaceutical Association, Harrisburg, Pa.:

So far the only cases prosecuted have been for laudanum.

From William H. McGarrah, president Pennsylvania Pharmaceutical Association, Scranton, Pa.:

Our association at each annual meeting appoints a committee to test or analyze all suspected adulterations. The result for a number of years has demonstrated that, with few exceptions, adulteration in drugs is not prevalent in this State. The committee has found that the powdered drugs were more frequently adulterated when competing with prices below the market value, the adulterant being an inert matter, usually cocoa-shell bark, powdered.

From Prof. Leffman, 715 Walnut street, Philadelphia, Pa.:

Some years ago the Dairymen's Protective Association of Pennsylvania, to which I have been acting as chemist, sent me samples of butter in small cakes (one-fourth pound), which was "stretched," that is, contained excess of water. It would lose considerable weight and shrink much on being kept a few days. It was made in the lower part of the city. I could get but little information about it, except that the so-called "cottage cheese" was used.

The Medical News, of January 28, 1893, contains the following table of analyses of malt extracts, made by Henry Leffmann, M. D., of Philadelphia:

Analytic notes on liquid malt extracts.

No.	Brand.	Claims.	Alcohol.	Solid ext. grms. to 100cc.	Salicylic acid.	Diastatic effect.
1	Blair's............	No alcohol...................	None.........	16.06	None.....	None.
2	Evans'............	Less than 4 per cent alcohol.	3 per cent.....	5.35	....do.....	Do.
3	Dukehart's.......	No alcohol...................	Present.......	25.22	Present...	Do.
4	Genois'..........	Less than 4 per cent alcohol.	6 per cent.....	15.4	None.....	Do.
5	Wyeth's..........	Less than 3 per cent alcohol.	2.98 per cent..	14.1	....do.....	Do.
6	Malt-Hopine.....	....	Present.......	8.97	Present...	Do.
7	Hercules	....................do	....do	10.23	None.....	Do.
8	English..........	Rich in extractive...........	....do	5.24	....do.....	Do.
9	Wampole's	A trifle over 4 per cent of alcohol.	7-7 per cent...	12.89	....do.....	Do.
10	Standard	Absolutely free from alcohol.	3 per cent.....	9.58	....do.....	Do.
11	Tarrant's........	....	Present.......	10.24	Present...	Do.
12	Johann Hoff's....	....	....do	8.44	None.....	Do.
13	"Trade".........	Highest per cent of extract and lowest of alcohol of any malt extract in use.	3 per cent.....	5.1	....do.....	Do.

The foregoing table does not require much comment. It is apparent from the assays that the liquid malt extracts are mostly beers; that they have but little if any value as either food or digestives, and that several of them are positively injurious. * * * I learn that at least one of the larger breweries makes a malt extract which is furnished in quantity. * * * I have designated this as "Trade" extract (No. 13). It apparently finds considerable sale.

As might be expected, no diastatic power was observed in any of the samples.

From Perry M. Gleine, druggist, 213 Rebecca street, Allegheny, Pa:

I am informed that the oil used in the manufacture of butterin is produced very largely here, and shipped extensively to Chicago, where it is used in manufacturing the same, none being made in this locality.

The law in this State prohibits the manufacture and sale of oleomargarin, but dealers still persist in selling the same, notwithstanding that the records of the court will show that there have been over 500 prosecuted for violating the law while protected, as they thought, by paying an internal-revenue fee.

Regarding cheese, it is not manufactured in this market, large quantities being shipped here from Chicago. Consequently we have no information on the adulteration of the same.

To the best of my knowledge and belief, children's foods, dairy, and pharmaceutical preparations, are sold strictly pure and up to the standard. We have a State pharmacy law which prohibits these adulterations, a State board empowered to prosecute violators, composed of five members, reputable pharmacists, of ten years' and more experience in the drug business.

From G. A. Hampson, secretary of Pennsylvania Cider and Jelly Makers' Association, North East, Pa.:

The extent to which the adulteration of vinegar and jellies is carried is almost beyond belief. Fully four-fifths of all the vinegar of the commerce of the United States to-day is made from something else than apple juice and is artificially colored to resemble cider vinegar. This is one of the primary causes of the decadence of the apple orchards throughout the country. The Pennsylvania State Cider and Jelly Makers' Association, of which I am secretary, at their last session pledged themselves to work for the enforcement and securing of a national food and drug law, compelling the branding of all articles. Jellies of all kinds are also extensively adulterated; and it goes without saying that such adulteration is exceedingly deleterious to health. Furthermore, without some law properly enforced it is difficult for the honest manufacturer to compete with fraud and colored goods. We have a vinegar law in Pennsylvania, but there is no provision made for the enforcement of same. Consequently it is practically a dead letter. We are satisfied that nothing short of a national law will effectively afford relief.

The extent to which scientific adulteration in vinegar and jellies is carried is fast freezing out the honest manufacturers, and soon there will be few pure goods left on the market.

In behalf of the Pennsylvania Cider and Jelly Makers' Association we earnestly urge the passage of a national pure-food law. Certainly no honest man can oppose the passage of such a law; but the immense capital engaged in adulteration will doubtless bring no end of pressure to defeat such law. In 1879 Congress passed a law granting the privilege of making low wines or weak whisky for vinegar-making without the payment of any revenue tax whatever. The effects of this law have been most disastrous.

The mills making this whisky vinegar are fitted up distillery fashion and are always located in the larger cities. The vinegar made from this weak whisky is in its natural state absolutely colorless, resembling water. But it is artificially colored to resemble cider vinegar, and is branded and sold throughout the country as cider vinegar. This vinegar is made principally from corn, but there is also a small admixture of rye. This corn vinegar can be made at a cost of 2 cents a gallon, and after it is colored to resemble cider vinegar, is sold at a price with which the honest cider-maker can not compete. But the cider-maker and orchardist are not the only sufferers.

The consumers are slowly poisoned by this artificially colored product and don't know what ails them. When Congress passed the iniquitous vinegar law of 1879 the numerous cider mills throughout the country began to go to the wall. There is not one cider mill now where there used to be five. It was a long time before the average cider-maker discovered what was the matter with his business.' He looked on in helpless wonder at those fellows from the cities with their wonderfully cheap vinegar and such prodigious quantities of it. But he discovered finally what was the matter, and for years has been trying to undo what Congress did 1879.

A bill has been introduced in Congress at every session since that time looking to the repeal of this law, but the corn men have defeated it every time. We tried to get the Paddock pure-food bill passed, but without success. It was fought bitterly by the vast capital of the country invested in the business of adulteration.

From Hugo Andriessen, druggist, Beaver, Pa.:

My next door corner grocery store neighbor sells his "pure powdered spices," put up in attractive packages, cheaper than I can purchase the whole spices at lowest wholesale rates.

He can afford to sell "pure extract vanilla" in large handsome bottles, artistically labeled, at 10 cents a bottle, while I, leaving the Tonca bean out, have to charge 25 cents, and let the trade go to the dishonest dealers. These few illustrations, I believe, suffice. It is the same with butter (oleomargarin), pure whisky (blended, compound-flavored spirits), wines, and even tinctures, extracts, and other articles of the United States Pharmacopœia.

From William B. Thompson, 4804 Trinity Place, Philadelphia, Pa.:

I know of no law on our statute books which provides penalties for the adulteration of food and drugs. The only condemnation which flagrant and obvious instances elicit, is the meager privilege of returning the rejected article to the seller with a feeble remonstrance against the sale of immature flesh, that which is known as "monkey veal" and damaged food material.

Every State pharmacy law has a clause or clauses against the adulteration of drugs and medicine, but there is no provision made for punishment. That which is everybody's business to expose and detect seems to be the business or concern of nobody, hence the evil continues.

That there does exist, to a very great and hurtful extent, systematic adulteration and admixture in drugs, an attenuation and criminal dilution of many domestic and household remedies in medicines, a willful compounding of inert substances with spices, and a mean mingling of worthless stuff with articles of prepared food, no observing or well-informed person can or will deny. Therefore, whatever may be the merit or demerit of the Paddock bill, do let us have something in the way of law that will protect against the mercenary avarice and greed of wicked and unscrupulous persons.

From Charles W. Hancock, druggist, Philadelphia, Pa.:

There seems to be an honest desire on the part of retail pharmacists to procure and sell those preparations that are standard, and this desire is increasing, though there have been a few instances lately where the officers of the State pharmaceutical examining board had several parties arrested and bound over at court for selling laudanum not up to the United States Pharmacopœia standard.

SOUTH CAROLINA.

From S. J. Duffie, druggist, Columbia, S. C.:

The adulteration of food and drugs in this State is carried on to a considerable extent, but there being no officers nor local laws to restrict same, I can not give any reliable data bearing on the subject. However, I am convinced, from a little observation of a personal nature, that a law on the same would be a great remedy for the worthless products which are now carried from place to place and sold in disguise. A great many preparations, such as laudanum, paregoric, etc., instead of containing the amount of opium prescribed by the pharmacopœia, have in their composition an amount insufficient to do any good whatever. There are a great many preparations which are thus weakened, and I am sure they endanger the lives of the people who take them. Such a case, if brought into court and proved, in all likelihood would be thrown out on the cry of jealousy, but if we had a national law on the subject and parties to enforce same, I am positive of good results. This is a subject in which I have taken a great deal of interest, but having no law to back me, have given up.

VERMONT.

From W. W. Cooke, director State Agricultural Experiment Station, Burlington, Vt.:

In Vermont there is no law concerning the adulteration of food and drugs, except a single statute relating to watering or skimming milk delivered at creameries or cheese factories, or retailed on the streets. This law has been quite rigidly enforced during the last three or four years, and has very largely decreased the extent to which this adulteration has been carried. There are no local laws in this State bearing on this subject. I should be very much in favor of a national food and drug law, provided one could be framed that would at all hit the necessities of the case.

MAPLE SUGAR.

From Hon. H. M. Haynes, internal-revenue agent, Montpelier, Vt.:

Vermont has a stringent law against adulteration of maple sugar, and as all such adulterations must be done secretly and in fear of penalty, it is not a matter admitting of statistical statement any more than illegal liquor selling or any other statutory violation. In my special work here in connection with maple-sugar bounty, however, I have endeavored to gather information in regard to this practice, and will summarize the results and my conclusions:

(1) I do not think the practice of adulterating maple sugar is nearly as extensive

as many people who have not made the study of it suppose. It is not easy in this comparatively sparsely settled State for a sugar-maker to lay in a supply of sugar other than maple, in quantities large enough to make extensive adulterations, without making himself an object of suspicion.

(2) Whatever adulteration has been or is done is not, as is supposed by the uninitiated, with low-grade cane sugar and glucose, but with refined or granulated sugars. This, mixed with dark and low-grade maple sugar, tends to lighten it in color and texture, and correspondingly increases its market value. I am satisfied that but an extremely small proportion of the sugar as it leaves the makers in this State contains anything but pure maple. It is a well-known fact, however, that great quantities of low-grade maple sugar, made from the last runs of sap, rank, woody, dark, and commanding a price of not more than 5 cents in the market, is bought up by manipulators in the large cities, worked over, purified, and adulterated, and thrown on the market the following spring as "genuine maple sugar," weeks before any maple sugar has been produced in the maple-sugar districts. This is a fraud on the purchaser who thinks he is buying new maple sugar, although the preparation he buys is infinitely more palatable and quite as good for the stomach as the cheap maple which is the basis of the preparation. The cheap stuff thus manipulated amounts to hundreds, possibly thousands, of tons each year.

WEST VIRGINIA.

From C. C. Brown, secretary of State Board of Agriculture, Charleston, W. Va.:

We think a national law governing food and drug adulteration would prove a great blessing to our people.

From Dr. J. W. McCoy, health officer, Wheeling, W. Va.:

I have just learned that some farmers living close to this city have recently brought an action against vendors of oleomargarin, who sold it contrary to law in this State, the law requiring the product to be colored pink.

From Hon. H. M. Turner, Shepherdstown, W. Va.:

I think a national pure-food bill should be passed and all food adulterations in this way lessened if not entirely broken up.

From B. F. Irons, M. D., Pickaway, W. Va.:

There is one matter that needs correction in our State, viz, whisky adulteration. Our druggists as a rule keep a very inferior and, in my opinion, badly adulterated whisky. I often get whisky for my patients that they can not use and have to send to another State for it, and I would be glad to see a national law which would compel the druggists to use or sell nothing but pure whisky.

WISCONSIN.

From Prof. Andrew S. Mitchell, analytical chemist, Milwaukee, Wis.:

In 1890 I caught a milkman adding annotto to skimmed milk and got a confession. Last week I received a barley that I believe to have been bleached with SO_2 fumes. Four years ago, when cocoa leaves were very high in price, I purchased two samples in different stores and neither contained one cocoa leaf. This leaf has two faint false ribs parallel to mid rib, and is characteristic.

I know of "coffee extract" containing no coffee and no chicory. I also have some flour-paste coffee-beans that are very natural in appearance. In ten samples of powdered opium assayed for morphine two fell far below 12 per cent and two others scant 12. I have names of makers and details. Tinctures of expensive drugs when prepared for country trade, and where competition is lively, very seldom are up to grade. A house in this city mixes ground flaxseed to order for any price. We have a good State food and dairy commission here, and they keep at work and get convictions, but they have more than their hands full with the dairy work alone

From R. Sauerhering, pharmacist, Mayville, Wis.:

No adulteration is practiced by our farmers, although sometimes stones are embedded in a tub of butter to increase the weight, which hardly can be classed an adulteration. It is clearly fraud.

From D. L. Harkness, dairy and food commissioner, of Wisconsin:

MILK.

It is now generally recognized that the only way to market milk, and especially where it is sold to cheese factories or creameries, is to sell it by the ratio of butter fat that it contains.

Selling milk regardless of quality for the purpose of making butter or cheese is just as absurd as selling hogs by the dozen the same as eggs. The ingredient that determines the value of the milk is the butter fat, and it is not only unbusiness-like, but unjust and unlawful, that a man who skims and waters his milk should receive the same price for an article that contains but 2½ per cent as the man who delivers a clean, unadulterated article containing 4 or 5 per cent of butter fat.

If no tests are made of the milk received at a cheese factory or creamery, the only gauge the manager has to follow is the number of pounds of cheese or butter that all the milk delivered makes, and if he pays the different patrons on this basis, the man who delivers good milk is paid no more than the man who previously removes a portion of the cream and converts it to his own use, or makes it into butter and sells it on the market.

The use of the Babcock test in the factory will remove this objection, and if payment is made upon the actual results of the tests, each man is paid for exactly what he delivers, and, moreover, the farmer who persistently waters or skims his milk is soon detected and is laid liable to the law for the deception that he endeavors to practice.

The standard adopted by the State, namely, 3 per cent of butter fat, is none too high, and it has been the experience of the members of this commission that the standard might be raised to 3½ per cent and do no injustice to the large majority of the patrons of our creameries and cheese factories.

SUGARS.

It is an open secret that almost every granulated sugar on the market is more or less adulterated with glucose, if with nothing more harmful, and it is such gigantic frauds as this that merit the attention of everyone that is interested in the adoption of laws that will compel the huge corporations that put forth such necessary articles of consumption to regard the health and legal rights of the public.

DRUGS.

In reviewing the various forms of adulteration the falsification and adulteration of drugs can not be too strongly condemned. It should be regarded as a far more heinous crime than the cheapening of some of the commoner articles of daily consumption.

We employ drugs only in the cases of direst necessity, and upon their action many times hang by slender threads the lives of those who are dear to us.

For instance, the doctor gives his patient a carefully calculated dose of henbane, and not receiving the result that he anticipated increases the dose until he gets the desired effect. Perhaps in this instance his patient recovers, and the good doctor, believing his druggist is the soul of honor—as indeed he is, for adulteration is seldom practiced among the retailers—makes a mental note of the fact that the patient has a peculiar idiosyncrasy in that he needs a much larger dose of henbane than that commonly given to obtain any benefit from it. Let us suppose that this patient has a relapse and once more calls the doctor. The medical man instantly remembers that he gave a very large dose of henbane in his former treatment before the disease succumbed, and he now decides to at once give what would appear to be a dangerous dose. He does so and sends the prescription to the druggist, who in the meantime has procured some of the solid extract of the drug that has not passed through the tender hands of the sophisticator, and he compounds the physician's prescription from this new supply. The patient takes it, his symptoms become alarming, and he may even die, and all the doctor can do is to marvel at the peculiarities of this man, who could take an extremely large dose of henbane in June, but who was poisoned by precisely the same dose in July.

Although the purpose and scope of this commission is better understood than formerly, still letters are received stating that samples have been forwarded for analysis and asking that the bill for the work be sent to the consignor.

COFFEES.

Of late years spurious coffees have appeared upon the market and are advertised openly without any attempt to conceal either their composition or purpose.

The prices quoted on these imitations are astonishingly low, being in one case 6 cents per pound in small lots and 5½ cents in barrel lots. These artificial coffee beans are made in close imitation of the genuine article, and taken in their unmixed state would deceive the eye of the most skillful observer. Upon a mere cursory examination the most particular housewife would pronounce them to be coffee beans of an excellent color and good roast. Without doubt the most common adulterant of coffee is chicory, but these coffee "pellets," as they are sometimes called, are fast supplanting chicory on account of their smaller cost. The pellets are composed of rye or wheat flour, are moulded in the shape of the genuine bean and held together by means of glucose or some similar vehicle, and are colored in imitation of a roasted coffee. Of course they have none of the properties of coffee, nor do they resemble it either in taste or smell, but when mixed with the genuine article, even in so large a quantity as 30 or 40 per cent, they are not easily detected except by expert examination.

It is not an uncommon practice to treat inferior or damaged coffees by some process for the improvement of their appearance and in imitation of superior grades. Java seems to have been especially subject to this treatment, or rather other coffees are colored in imitation of Java. South American coffees are often exposed to a high, moist heat, which changes their color from green to brown, thus forming imitation Java.

Various pigments are also used in coloring coffees. The Division of Chemistry of the U. S. Department of Agriculture found as high as one-twenty-fourth grain of Scheele's green in one-half ounce of coffee. Scheele's green is a combination of copper and arsenious acid, both violent poisons. Yellow ocher, silesian blue, chrome yellow, burnt umber, Venetian red, drop black, charcoal, and French black have been used to color coffees, and it is polished by rotation in cylinders with soapstone. Raw coffees which have been damaged by sea water are washed, decolorized with limewater, again washed, rapidly dried, and colored by a slight roasting by azo-orange. By this method Santos coffees are converted into imitation Javas. The weight lost is regained by steaming and then coating the beans with glycerin, palm oil, or vaseline to prevent evaporation.

Coffees are sometimes faced with Prussian blue or indigo, lead chromate, etc. The following list of facing mixtures is from the published investigations of K. Sykora: First, mixture of indigo, lead chromate, coal, and clay; second (approximately), 5 parts indigo, 10 parts coal, 4.5 parts lead chromate, 65.5 parts clay, and 15 parts ultramarine; third (approximately), 5 parts indigo with some yellow dye, 3 parts coal, 8 parts lead chromate, 82 parts clay, 2 parts ultramarine; fourth (approximately), 12 parts indigo, and some yellow dye, 5.5 parts coal, 4.5 parts lead chromate, 6.6 parts clay, and 12 parts ultramarine.

The most criminal part of adulteration of this sort is that the cheapest classes of goods suffer the most and the very people who can least afford to be preyed upon are the very ones at whom these acts are directed. The dealer who caters to those in the humbler walks of life is nine times out of ten compelled to sell his wares at a merely nominal profit, and unless he is shrewd enough and firm enough to refuse to extend credit he suffers by the loss of accounts that he has allowed to run or been unable to collect, and to compensate himself for this loss he often resorts to substitution and adulteration. Many articles that in themselves are not deleterious are sold fraudulently and in these instances it is the aim of the laws of this State and the endeavor of this commission to protect not only the health but also the pocketbooks of the people of Wisconsin.

Another method that is used to defraud the innocent purchaser is the so-called "sweating" of coffee and spices. The coffee or spice is subjected to a process of extraction whereby the essential oils and other principles are removed, and after being reroasted and colored, and in some instances chemically doctored to impart something of its original flavor, it is put upon the market as being genuine and sold as such. This process, of course, allows the dishonest dealer to reap two profits upon each lot of goods. It is especially employed in the extraction of the vital principle of coffee, of most of the spices that have an acrid oil, as mustard, and also upon the various sources of the flavoring extracts, especially upon the vanilla bean.

The most of the flavoring extracts upon the market, and more especially those exhibiting the qualities of the tropical fruits, the banana, pineapple, etc., are prepared from ethers and artificial flavoring agents that are certainly most injurious. The so-called "almond" flavoring extract is made in many cases from the oil of mirbane or from nitrobenzol, both of which are exceedingly poisonous.

The writer has occupied his present position since September 1, 1892, and in that time the samples of milk that we have received, numbering about 1,500; have made an excellent average. Recently we have been doing considerable work in the enforcement of our vinegar laws, and in this field we find much need of attention, the principal violations being the sale of brown goods for cider, and the sale of goods that run below 4 per cent in acetic acid, there being but few cases where mineral acids have been added. Other food products have exhibited the usual run of adulteration.

The members of our commission are the only State officials charged with the duty of enforcing the laws against the adulteration of foods and drugs, other than the State board of health and the State board of pharmacy.

Teas, coffees, spices, baking powders, and, in fact, almost all of the culinary supplies are adulterated in many instances, and the average consumer is not in a position to determine when he is defrauded, nor is he in a position to successfully resent the deception were he able to detect it.

From Andrew S. Mitchell, analytical chemist and assayer, 436 Milwaukee street, Milwaukee, Wis.:

We need national supervision of the sale of food and drugs; and the supervision must come from experts who are specialists, and they must be beyond the reach of politics.

Adulteration is common in almost all branches of trade.

I have found boracic acid in milk and have had one skimmed sample that was colored with annotto.

There is very little cider vinegar here that is not low wine vinegar colored with caramel. I have at present samples of cheese made from skimmed milk to which have been added margarine fats to replace the butter removed. Under the State law these can not be sold without branding, so the makers consign them to themselves in Chicago, Ill. When they arrive there they are placed on the market there as they have no one appointed to enforce their laws.

I have met the paste coffee bean and "black pepsin" for butter. Spices are all more or less reduced. I worked on one ginger a short time ago, and found turmeric and wheat flour.

From George S. Cox, State chemist, Wisconsin dairy and food commission, Madison, Wis.:

The Wisconsin dairy and food commission is testing about 600 samples of various food products in the laboratory each month. Many of these are milk samples, and since the commission began operations, about four years ago, marked improvements have become apparent in the quality of the milk that is offered for sale, both to the creameries and cheese factories and also for private consumption. Inspections have been made in the larger cities of Wisconsin and it is safe to say that whole milk is very generally sold in this State.

Recently there has been considerable agitation of the vinegar question with us. Our laws require 4 per cent of acetic acid in all vinegars and 2 per cent of cider solids in all cider vinegars and make the sale of a vinegar below this standard a misdemeanor, punishable by a fine of from $10 to $100. The department has made a number of prosecutions under this law since the opening of the year, with beneficial results. When active operations were commenced in this line, about 50 per cent of the vinegars sold in the State did not comply with this law. This was mainly due to the manufacturers, who, having enjoyed immunity from interference, continued to ship into Wisconsin goods that could not be sold elsewhere When the vinegar law was passed in 1891, immediate steps were taken to notify all manufacturers and dealers in vinegar of its provisions, and samples were frequently taken at various points and were reported upon in order to bring the law into greater prominence. After these premonitory measures, suits were commenced against some of those who were violating the statute, and in all cases, excepting one, the parties either entered a plea of guilty or were convicted as charged. In all instances where the vinegar had been supplied them by a reliable house the fines, which were made as low as possible, were refunded by the wholesaler and, as the expense came out of the wholesaler or manufacturer, they at once took steps to send nothing but legal vinegar into the State.

At present many of the retail dealers throughout the State make a practice of sending small samples of every lot of vinegar purchased to the commission, where it is analyzed and reported upon free of any charge to them, and they are thus enabled to guarantee their customers a legal article and, at the same time, to protect themselves against the unscrupulous manufacturer.

On the whole the work of the department has been beneficial, but these benefits to the people have been somewhat curtailed by the lack of laws that can be readily enforced.

The Wisconsin laws fix an arbitrary standard for three articles of food only, viz, vinegar, milk, and cheese. In regard to other food products and drugs, it lies with the commissioner and his assistants to prove that the substance in question is injuriously adulterated.

In many instances it is impossible to do this, as, in the eyes of the average jury, a substance is injurious only when its deleterious effects are immediate and apparent.

The commission consists of a commissioner, dairy expert, and the State chemist. Chapter 452. Laws of Wisconsin, 1889, clearly defines the duties and powers of these officers, but, with the exceptions above cited, the laws they are charged with enforcing are almost inoperative. The law regulating the sale of drugs is a notable instance, but it is so framed that a conviction is almost an impossibility, and in the eleven years that it has been on the statute books there has not been one instance of a conviction under it. Nevertheless, it is hardly possible that there are no adulterated drugs in Wisconsin.

The members of the commission framed a bill that was introduced into the legislature of this year, but it died in the hands of a committee after vigorous opposition from some of the leading drug firms of the State.

This measure was practically a copy of the laws now in force in Ohio, New York, and New Jersey, and, like the laws of these States, referred the standard of drugs to the United States Pharmacopoeia.

The writer had occasion several times to champion the measure and found the great objection to the section that treated upon drugs to be as follows: It was argued that if the bill became a law and any drug should differ very slightly from the prescribed limits of the Pharmacopoeia, the druggist dispensing the same would be liable to a prosecution maliciously instituted by a business rival or a personal enemy. While this objection seems to carry some weight upon its face, it must be remembered that the Pharmacopoeia itself permits some variability in drugs, and in the matter of a tincture, for example, before a suit could be tried, its strength or quality would necessarily have to be determined by a chemist or other expert, and to him it would quickly become apparent whether the article had been fraudulently tampered with or whether the variation from the standard was an unavoidable one and originated through some natural cause and by no fault of the maker.

The members of this commission are strongly in favor of a law that will " compel the branding of articles of food and drugs shipped from one State into another."

The need of such a law is daily apparent in our work. We can have recourse upon a manufacturer within the confines of our State who makes spurious goods, but if he locates just over the State line we can direct our attacks upon his goods only against the retailer, who is generally innocent of any intent to deceive his customers and is himself a victim of the manufacturer.

From W. F. Montgomery, druggist and pharmacist, Appleton, Wis.:

In cheese-making there is some cream or brick cheese made with old butter, poor cheese, and a little cream to work them up with, which gives it the beautiful odor usually found around a free-lunch counter.

In regard to children's food, all the dry food on the market that I have seen and tested is all right. But it must be kept air-tight and in a cool, dry place. All the condensed milks or foods in market are dangerous articles for the use of children. In fact, the Government had better offer a premium to every mother to feed her children in the natural way; our country would grow physically, hence mentally.

Most of the cry of adulteration of infants' foods throughout the country is made by poor M. D. quacks and cranks. When called to see children that are ailing, not having ability to diagnose the disease, they add more to the little child's suffering by advising the mother to change the food, and then if the child dies, the last food given was adulterated, so as to let the doctor out.

From George E. Banks, Tomah, Wis.:

As to adulteration, I find marked instances in commercial cream of tartar, bicarbonate of soda, and so-called olive oils.

From C. W. Wright, druggist, Platteville, Wis.:

There is a large amount of butter color used here.

I have made but few examinations of drugs for adulterations, as my original work has been in organic chemistry. The only cases that have come under my notice are as follows:

(1) Gum asafetida, in which small pieces of flint were used to represent the " tears " of the true gum. At least 50 per cent of the sample I had was earthy matter.

(2) Glycerin, such brands as are usually quoted at about 14 or 15 cents a pound. I

have examined several that were marked "chemically pure," "for medicinal purposes," and found that they nearly all showed the presence of cane sugar. The test used was that of the United States Pharmacopœia, 1890.

(3) Wintergreen herb. This sample was the worst I had ever seen. It had the appearance of having been taken from a henhouse, and it was so poor a substitute for wintergreen herb that I returned it to the house I got it from without making any other examination.

From E. F. Ramsland, Westly, Wis.:

Children's foods are nearly all patent or proprietary articles that may be classed as secret nostrums. Some of them are fairly good, but most of them are of an uncertain composition.

Pharmaceutical preparations are very largely adulterated, particularly common commercial preparations, and especially powdered drugs. Many druggists make a practice of preparing common preparations of an inferior strength. For instance, I might cite that spirits nitrous ether is made in many places with alcohol and water in equal quantities, and when thus made it quickly deteriorates. It occurs frequently in the market containing only 1 or 2 per cent of the ethyl nitrite($C_2H_5NO_2$), instead of 5 per cent, as the Pharmacopœia directs. For the dispensing of physicians' prescriptions I usually find a better grade of goods kept in stock.

From George W. Corbett, Plymouth, Wis.:

I have examined several samples of mustard and found nearly all to contain ocher.

3183—No. 41——4

Following is a list of some foods and drugs, arranged alphabetically, the ordinary sophistications of each article being given under the appropriate head:

Absinthe.—Undistilled liquors (from beet). Damaged and inferior material, to which is added aromatic resins. benzoins, guaiacum, etc.

Alcohol.—Methyl alcohol made from wood is largely used in adulterations.

Alcoholic liquors.—Fusil oil, tannin, logwood, water, coloring matter, burnt sugar.

Kirschwasser (German cherry brandy) is imitated by a compound of apricot and cherry seed, peach leaves dried, myrrh, and alcohol.

Gin (rye whisky and barley). potatoes and barley, alum, spirits of turpentine, sugar, and water.

Ales, English and American.—Many people prefer English ale. Now, whether this is because of its superiority or because it is "English" is a question that the writer does not pretend to decide. It is a fact that the imported article costs more, and as some people grade what they buy by the price, probably the preference is due to the increased cost. If this be so, and no one can dispute it, the purchaser of the imported and higher priced article, is entitled to get the genuine article, and when imported ales are mixed with the American product and sold as genuine, the fact of such a sale, while neither improving nor lowering the quality of the ale, doubtless lowers the standard of honesty, and is without doubt a fraud, and commercially an adulteration. The fact that over 30 qualities of ale are sold in England should lead the purchaser to inquire which quality he purchases when he buys the "real article" on this side of the water. An interesting notice on this subject in the New York Analyst points out these and other facts, to wit, that the bottler often fails to allow ale to ripen in the casks before confining it in bottles, and lastly the writer points out that the clearest and most transparent ale is not always the most desirable. In England people do not drink as cold drinks as we do, and an English beer brewed to use with their temperature of consumption would grow cloudy when put in the American ice box.

Ammonia.—When used in bread or cake to whiten and lighten flour is injurious and should be prevented.

Baking powders.—Alum for cream of tartar, starch in undue quantities, coarse hominy. Alum is often used to liberate carbonic acid, although not an acid salt. Its use in so-called cream of tartar baking powders is clearly an adulteration. In several States its use in baking powders is prohibited except when distinctly branded on the label. Alum in baking powders, when branded as required by law, in some States can not be considered an adulteration, as there is no official standard, but when sold as cream of tartar powders the use is certainly fraudulent, and the article an adulterant.

Beer.—Burnt sugar, licorice, treacle, quassia, coriander and caraway seed, Cayenne pepper, soda, salicylic acid, salt, carbonic gas (artificially injected), grains other than barley, glycerin, glucose, water (by retailers) tobacco, and seed of *coculus indicus.*

Black pepper.—Buckwheat flour and hulls, P. D. cracker crumbs, corn meal, wheat flour, charcoal, sand, bran, linseed meal, cocoanut shells, mustard seed hulls, sawdust, olive stones, Cayenne pepper, red clay, and ship bread. There is hardly anything of a refuse character that is not used by manufacturers to adulterate pepper.

Bread.—Alum, sulphate of copper, ammonia, inferior flour, and corn meal and rye flours.

Butter.—Oleomargarin, butterin, water (stretched butter) in undue proportions, lard, alkalines and rancid butter, cotton oil, beef suet, olive oil.

Candy.—Tartaric acid is used to cut the sugar and prevent granulation. Glucose is used on account of its cheapness to the extent of 10 or 20 per cent. Being less sweet than sugar it is a deterioration and is, therefore, undoubtedly an adulterant. Chrome yellow, soapstone, terra alba, baryta, and starch, are all used to a greater or less extent.

Cider.—"Country cider," so called, is made by the following method. Such cider, (?) of course, depreciates the market value of apples, and is not as healthful nor as palitable as the old-fashioned sort:

To each gallon of water add one-half pound of granulated sugar, acidulate with tartaric acid and flavor with oil of apple, previously put in alcohol; color with caramels, and to 20 gallons of this mixture add 2 gallons of genuine country cider.

Dried apples.—Zinc and copper, weighted with water and sirup and water.

Eggs.—The yolks of eggs are now largely imitated, and it is stated that the whole egg is now successfully duplicated as a result of scientific genius.

Glucose.—It is a clear, transparent, stiff-flowing liquid, which is made from corn by the use of sulphuric acid. It is not as sweet as sugar, and costs 2 to 3 cents per pound, or about one-half the price of sugar. It is used largely in the adulteration of candy, sirup, beer, and jelly. Dr. W. P. Toury says of this article:

A skilled confectioner told me he considered glucose in any kind of candy unnecessary, injurious to health, and unquestionably an adulterant.

Glycerin.—Glucose, water.

Infant foods.—Many of the so-called milk foods contain but little, and some no, milk. These foods are principally made from wheat, differently prepared.

Mace.—Venetian red mixed with baked cracker or bread dust.

Spices.—The London Confectioner says:

In some cases the essential oils are even extracted from pure spices prior to grinding.

It is generally believed that the same practice is carried on to a large extent in this country not only with spices but with coffee.

Shrimps.—Colored with Venetian red.

Seidlitz powder.—Short weight, Epsom salts, and Glauber salts.

Soaps.—According to the Pharmaceutical Examiner, the German soap-makers have directed attention to the frequent adulteration in soap. The most common adulterants used are said to be starch, flour, tallow, spar, salt, mineral lubricating oil, and excess of water.

Water.—Lead from lead pipes is a fruitful source of bad health and should be carefully guarded against.

A rough but reliable method to detect lead in water is to add a few drops of acetic acid to 10 ounces of the water contained in a pint stoppered bottle, and a grain or two of bichromate of potash, and shake well. If the water contains lead it becomes opaque, through the formation of bichromate of lead.

Wine.—The following is of interest in connection with the subject of wine adulteration:

The British consul at Cadiz states that he and a friend, visiting one of the native sherry cellars there, were given two samples of wine to drink, which seemed to be almost identical, and were told that one was a natural product, and very costly ($250, equal to £50, a bottle), while the other was a manufactured product, the market price of which was only a few cents a bottle. In making the imitation the natural product is first analyzed, and the chemist, ascertaining the exact nature of its constituent parts, is able to combine them, and thus nearly reproduce the original compound.

MISCELLANEOUS INFORMATION RELATING TO FOOD ADULTERATION.

ADULTERATED BEER.

The Indianapolis Right and Freedom, of April 1, 1893, says that an educated and wealthy German attributes American suicides to adulterated beer, and declares that the adulterants used "have a depressing effect on the nervous system and dispose the subject to melancholy." Chemically pure beer will produce no such effect. It will be remembered in this connection that Germany prohibits the use of salicylic acid in beer to be used in the Fatherland, but allows its use in beer made for export.

POISONED BY TINNED BEEF.

A family residing at Chelmsford partook of some American corned beef for breakfast on the morning of Wednesday, March 27. The meat was observed to be slightly moist on the surface and did not drop out of the tin readily. It is also stated that the meat had a "spicy" flavor, as of thyme. The mother, who is an elderly lady, about an hour and a half after breakfast complained of feeling giddy, and shortly afterward persistent vomiting supervened, followed by cramps, spasms, and diarrhea. The father, son, daughter, and a maidservant were attacked shortly after, and for a time the life of the son was despaired of. All have now recovered. Unfortunately the remaining meat was destroyed. This, of course, is to be regretted, as in all such cases the unconsumed portion should be reserved for chemical and bacterilogical examination. When examined a few days later the under surface of the tin was found to be corroded considerably more than was the case with the other tins which had been kept a much longer time. In the scrapings of fat from the side of the tin both lead and tin were detected by Dr. Thresh. The symptoms, however, were undoubtedly those of ptomaine poisoning.—*American Analyst.*

THE RETAILER NOT ALWAYS TO BLAME.

Here is proof positive that the Massachusetts Health Board prefers to bring cases against the manufacturers and big houses rather than the retailers. Will the Merchant's Review make a note of it? If we had a national food law what a scampering to get under cover there would be by the out-of-the-State frauds. Israel Renaud, a wholesale grocer of Fall River, Mass., was arraigned in the district court on a charge of violating the food laws by selling maple sirup which had been adulterated with glucose. State Inspector McCaffry and his assistant had purchased a can of the sirup of a retail dealer. He informed them that he had purchased it of a Mr. Renaud. The defense made a stubborn fight and contended that the goods were marked as "compound" and not sold as pure, but the court found the defendant guilty and ordered him to pay a fine of $25 and costs. An appeal was taken and the case will go to a higher court.—*American Analyst, June 1, 1893.*

ADULTERATION OF DAIRY PRODUCTS.

Hon. James H. Brown, of the New York State dairy commission, in an address before the sixteenth annual session of the New York Dairymen's Association, (p. 178, of report) said:

Our cities and towns were at that time flooded with adulterated milk, butter, and cheese, which tended toward discredit and distrust of the New York State products, and lessened their consumption, as the goods used were so adulterated that the product of the dairyman entered but a little way in their manufacture. This condition of affairs would soon have driven our farmer entirely out of business, and when he is oppressed or depressed all people of the State must suffer. Without him we can not live; and thus it was, that with chalk and water for milk, lard, tallow, and horse grease for butter, and cheese enriched with lard, the farmer was certainly in a very bad predicament. With this serious state of affairs confronting our land, our homes, and our prosperity, it became necessary that something be done immediately. Our legislature passed and our governor immediately signed the act, and appointed as the first New York State dairy commissioner the gentleman who still holds that office. I hardly think our legislators had well-defined ideas of what this department could do, what it would do, or what it should do. They fully appreciated the fact that something prompt and decisive must be done, and so passed this law, believing it to be the best thing at that time appearing, and I think I am fully justified in saying that from later developments it has proved to be the best law for the producer and consumer of dairy products that could have been passed. Our department always has, and it always must have in order to succeed, the hearty cooperation of both the producer and consumer.

Our law has been amended and new duties added from time to time as experience suggested and necessity compelled, until at the present time the dairy commission is charged with the execution of the provisions of various laws which provide against the manufacture and sale of any article made in semblance or imitation of natural butter or cheese; against selling or offering for sale milk that is adulterated, unclean, or unwholesome; against branding cheese with a false brand; against the sale of adulterated vinegar, and also for a system of instruction to improve the quality of the butter and cheese manufactured in the State.

The commissioner became satisfied that the root of the oleomargarine evil was the retail dealer; he bought the goods knowing just what they were because they were cheap, but in all cases sold them to the consumer for dairy butter.

The commissioner therefore began with the retail dealer, arresting and prosecuting every one found, until the business became so risky that very few were willing to try the sale.

In 1883 there were upwards of 15,000,000 pounds of the article handled in this State, and to-day there is none sold for consumption, excepting possibly a very small amount clandestinely. It was ascertained that the enforcement of this law the first year reduced the sale of these goods fully 50,000 pounds per day. This implied, of course, the same number of pounds more of butter consumed. This has not been accomplished without a struggle and a hard, bitter fight.

The enforcement of the statute relating to milk has been followed up rigidly. The first year or two it was impossible to extend operations over the entire State, because of a lack of funds. We, therefore, confined our early inspections to New York, Brooklyn, and the surrounding counties. This was no small undertaking, as statistics show that in 1885 there were shipped into these cities alone 4,835,831 forty-quart cans of milk, and that this year 7,040,342 forty-quart cans have been received. Our first experience was that quite a large amount of this milk was of poor quality and that it arrived in poor shape, but by persistent work we are now able to say that dairy products reach the consumer in much better condition and with less adulteration than almost any other kind of food.

To illustrate how nearly absolutely pure our milk product is, we will state our recent experience. Desirous of knowing just how and in what condition as to purity the milk was when it reached New York city, we directed a sufficient number of experts to report to the assistant commissioner, having that territory in charge, so that he might be able to inspect all the milk received in these cities in one day. We inspected that morning 16,371 forty-quart cans and found only 88 of doubtful quality, showing only one-half of 1 per cent to have been adulterated.

It is also another noticeable fact that the milk delivered in these cities by parties residing outside of our State shows a much larger percentage of adulteration than our own production does, foreign milk showing 4 cans out of each 100 to be adulterated, while our own shows only three-fourths of 1 can. This is not only very gratifying to us as a department, but it speaks well for the integrity of our dairymen and creamery men.

The assistant commissioners are distributed in different portions of the State as judiciously as possible. An assistant in the country is able to superintend a much larger territory than one in the city, and is accordingly given a large division. There is an assistant at each of the following places: Albany, New York City, Washingtonville, Holland Patent, Lowville, Castile, Rochester, Buffalo, and Ellicottville. In this way we are able thoroughly and systematically to cover the whole State. We have also four cheese instructors, whose duty it is to go from place to place through the State, giving instruction and aid where needed, and to endeavor to make our cheese as nearly uniform as possible.

We have become satisfied that much of the poor cheese on the market is occasioned by poor care of the milk at the farm; hence, we have advocated the necessity and importance not only of cleanliness in the milking and surroundings, but of a thorough aëration of the milk at the farm instead of cooling in the usual way.

Aëration, however, has its dangers. We have found people who were faithfully using aërators in the cow barns, thus exposing their milk in the worst possible manner, and as a result the maker was obliged to call on us for aid. We traced the difficulty to two or three dairies and soon straightened the matter out by getting these people to use their aërators outside of the barn. I do not think nor does our experience show all trouble to be caused by the dairymen. The reports from some factories are perfectly astounding, and it seems almost incredible that any should think that good cheese could be made in such pens as are sometimes used, or with the implements with which they work. They expect our instructor to step into such a place, where he is an entire stranger, and make as fine an article as is to be found on the market; then, too, there are numbers in this State who are masquerading under the colors of cheese-makers when they are not competent or qualified to be a helper for some first-class maker.

The quality of cheese in this State is certainly improving, and we, as a department, claim our full share of the credit. We have a law relating to the branding of cheese, and the number of brands used is increasing each year. This is very gratifying to us. We are glad to note the fact that buyers often refuse to purchase cheese unless they bear the State brand, and in many cases will pay more for goods so stamped. Our uniform experience has been, that wherever we have been able to extend our operations, those interested have been unwilling that any of the force should be withdrawn, and insist that our work in their locality be increased.

It is stated that there has been consumed in the cities of New York and Brooklyn during the last year 363,388,840 quarts of milk, condensed milk, and cream, to say nothing about the number of quarts of milk required to make the large quantity of butter and cheese consumed by these cities.

We have taken a large number of samples of adulterated articles, made many arrests, and striven in every way to afford all the protection in our power, both to the honest producer and to the consumer. We have become satisfied and our experience demonstrates that the protection of the consumer against unwholesome, impure, and adulterated goods, and against frauds of all kinds in this line, as well as the

best interests of the honest dairyman himself, lies not so much in the fact of prose
cutions as it does in the important fact that there is a department whose special
duty it is to see that these laws are obeyed. No one knows when an agent of this
department will appear to test the product. Thus, from fear of detection the person
disposed to be dishonest will bring honest milk to our creameries, cheese factories,
and homes.

The vinegar law is the latest addition to our duties. We are following this up just
as we have done the others and are meeting with the very same resistance. We are
winning nearly all our suits, and we propose to stay by and fight it out on this line
until the trade becomes so unpleasant and unprofitable that no dealer can be found
willing to handle the goods.

At the same meeting the following proceedings also occurred:

A. R. EASTMAN. You remember last fall when the cholera was at our doors, the
people said something must be done to stop it, and the governor immediately went
to work, and he said: "Let us buy a quarantine station, and I know if it is bought
that the people of the State will pay for it." Why? Because it was to protect the
interests of the masses and not of individuals. The people will not hesitate to pay
taxes to protect our country from disease.

Now, we have another disease in this country that is even worse than cholera, if
we did but know it. It is backed up by millions, and it is trying to push itself into
the legislature of this State to break down the laws we have to-day. It is not as
potent on the surface as cholera, or as quick in its work, but it exists and its backers
are ready to throw it on the market; and it is oleomargarin and butterin. They
charge that the dairymen of the State are taking $90,000 or $95,000 to protect their
interests. But this is not true. It is to protect every man, woman, and child in
this State collectively and not as individuals. Now, this is a question that ought
to be considered.

The dairy commissioner's department is not a protection to dairymen alone, but it
is a protection to the masses. The power back of oleomargarin is money, and we
know what money can do. It is that class of men that are trying to break down
our law. Why? Because there are millions of money back of it. If they can
break down that commission, what have they got? In twenty-four hours they could
put oleomargarin on the market at 12 cents a pound, and there is millions in it.

I say we ought to stand by this department. That it has been ably conducted by
Mr. Brown is undisputed. And the strongest element against him to-day is the men
who stand ready in twenty-four hours to put butterin and oleomargarin upon the
market.

So I am glad Mr. Brown has given us that paper here, and has told us something
about the department and about the troubles they have to contend with.

Prof. BABCOCK. This subject of oleomargarin is something I really come very
little in contact with. Our own State is protected very much in the same way as
this State is, except not as thoroughly. In Wisconsin oleomargarin is permitted to
be sold under its proper name; that is, so long as it is not sold as butter. There is
no restriction further than that placed upon its sale. I do know, however, that this
weakness of the law, if I may be permitted to call it so, has allowed oleomargarin
to be sold throughout the State, but not under its proper name. As to the unhealth-
fulness of oleomargarin, I am well aware that there may be a great deal of unhealthful material put into a mass of that kind. How far it goes I do not know, as I have
not had opportunity to examine and of course have to accept the evidence as it is
offered. Whether it is true or not makes no difference to the general public. Every
one wants to get butter when he wants it. One does not want, under the guise of
butter, to get something else, whether it is just as good or not, or just as healthful.
There is a sentiment back of it which sustains them in their desires. Every one
wants to be protected in that line, be he rich or poor. There is not one person in a
thousand who, when he asks for butter is not willing to pay the difference between

butter and oleomargarin, and people do not want anything else foisted upon them, and the laws can not be too stringent in this regard. I believe the State of New York has been very wise in passing laws prohibiting the sale of oleomargarin in any form whatever. I believe laws of this kind are necessary to protect the dairy interests against its introduction, and I do not believe it can be done in any half way manner whatever. Nobody can deny that oleomargarin is a legitimate article of commerce so long as it is sold under its proper name, but you can not prevent its being sold very largely as butter. I do not believe it is possible to prevent oleomargarin taking the place of at least 30 per cent of the butter sold, but it will take its place at the price of butter; that is, they will sell oleomargarin under the name of butter; and I do not believe, furthermore, that under that plan it is possible to keep it out.

USE AND ADULTERATION OF MILK.

The Morning Oregonian, a paper that makes no mistakes when talking upon a subject in which its readers are directly interested, says:

The fight against butterin and oleomargarin is one that has been waged fiercely between those who desire to protect the human stomach from being made an unwilling receptacle for the cast-off oils and fats of pork houses, and those who see in the process an enormous pecuniary profit. Spurious butter, however attractive it may be made to appear, has only to be known by its name to be repudiated as containing all the possibilities of filth concealed by the cunning of the manufacturer from the perception of taste, sight, and smell.

Then comes the pepsin "racket," which is as follows: 1 pint of milk, 1 ounce of salt, 6 grains of pepsin, 12 grains of sodium sulphate, and 1 pound of butter. Warm the mixture to blood heat, then agitate or churn the mixture, and the result will be 2 pounds 1 ounce and 18 grains of good-looking butter. A glance at this compound will show that it is within a few ounces of being half water, and if it should happen that the pound of butter used had over 11 per cent water, then the compound would be half water.

As far back as history goes we find milk spoken of as a most important and palatable article of food, and in ancient times it was considered to contain many hidden virtues. Boerhave appears to have been the first to make a qualitative examination of milk, and speaks at some length on the danger of using milk from diseased or improperly fed animals. Milk is a fluid secreted by the mammary glands of animals for the support and nourishment of their young, and consists of an emulsion of fats in a solution of casein and sugar, together with certain inorganic salts. The color of milk is due to the fat globules, which can be readily seen with the aid of a microscope. It is claimed that 222,000,000 of these globules will not more than fill an inch square of space. Up to the seventeenth century only three of the constituents of milk had been discovered, viz, butter, cheese, and whey. Even birds and plants secrete a fluid similar in composition to milk. In civilized countries cow's milk is principally consumed; in Africa, that of the camel; in Tartary and Siberia, that of the mare; in India, the buffalo's; in Lapland, the reindeer's; in China, until a comparatively recent date, sow's milk was generally consumed. Milk is especially adapted for the support of the young of animals, because it contains all the components of a mixed food, each for its kind.

An examination of the needs of the body shows that definite amounts of carbon, hydrogen, nitrogen, and oxygen are required daily, depending on the amount lost by the body and the organs used. An excess beyond this is needed by the young animal to furnish material for growth. In milk, casein supplies the nitrogen; sugar and fat, in a great measure, the carbon; the salts, the mineral constituents; and the water, the water needed by the body. It is for this reason that cow's milk must be diluted before being given to infants, as the percentage of casein is too large. Should it not be diluted then the infant has to digest the excess of casein, and so give its digestive organs more work to do, thus permanently injuring them.

In this, as in many other countries, cow's milk is the sort used almost entirely, and when we consider that two-thirds of our infant population are brought up on other than human milk, viz, cow's, and that nearly all children partake more or less largely of cow's milk, to say nothing of its general use, we can at once see the necessity of a pure milk supply. This is particularly necessary when milk is used as substitute for mother's milk, for cow's milk, although the best we can get, is still different in its chemical properties and amounts of its constituents, and any adulterations only tends to increase this difference, and consequently its indigestibility is greater. As, for instance, in skim milk the per cent of fat is too small, while the per cent of casein is too large, or by adulteration with water the per cent of the solid constituents is lowered, and more of such milk must be digested in order that the body may obtain sufficient nourishment.

The adulteration of milk, however, is a question that needs special and careful attention, as it is not only one of the most important articles of diet, but is undoubtedly the most susceptible of being contaminated by the absorption of impurities from its surroundings, as well as being easily injured by the food given the cow, its purity depending largely upon what she eats and the water she drinks. The health of the animal is also another important question, as it is a well recognized fact that tuberculosis in the cow engenders it in the system of those who use the milk. For the reason that tuberculosis is known to be among the cattle in this State, I have asked Dr. Withycombe, our very competent State veterinarian, to supply me with a short paper. He says:

"Tuberculosis is the bane of the human family, and among the potent agencies in conveying this dangerous and subtle malady to children is milk. Recent scientific investigations have been the means of throwing much light on the propagation of tuberculosis. It is estimated by good authority that from 5 to 20 per cent of cows in the vicinity of large cities are affected with tuberculosis. It is not the proximity of the city which tends to the development of the disease, but it is altogether due to the conditions under which the animals are kept. Close confinement, improper ventilation, unwholesome food, long periods of heavy milking, are some of the evils which have a tendency to weaken the vitality of the cows and render them peculiarly susceptible to the disease. The great problem to solve at the present is, how can we detect the disease in the living subject with a certainty? Physical examination and microscopical inspection of milk have utterly failed to reveal the presence of the disease in numerous cases. 'According to Collinger, the milk of 11 out of 20 cows suffering from tuberculosis was infectious, although the actual bacilli could be discovered in but one sample.' The very best medical and veterinary experts, after a careful physical examination, failed to detect the presence of the disease in cows that were afterwards subjected to the Koch test, which test proved a complete success, the characteristic reaction and elevation, of temperature occurring in each case. Prof. Koch's lymph probably failed to accomplish and answer the purposes for which it was first intended, nevertheless it will probably prove to be the most valuable agent ever discovered to prevent the spreading of tuberculosis. Milk being largely the diet of children, this fact should remind us of the care and precaution we should exercise in furnishing this article of food free from death-breeding germs, especially the tubercular bacilli, which too often finds a suitable home in the delicate and sensitive tissues in the body of a child to execute its work of destruction."

At this point I would also call special attention to the care of milk after having been received by the consumers. We all understand that if a cow eats impure food or inhales impure air that her milk will be influenced thereby. No food seems so peculiarly qualified to absorb impurities that come in contact with it as milk. So long as milk is warmer than the atmosphere, it is quite safe, for in that condition it resists and throws off approaching danger, but as soon as it becomes colder than the atmosphere, it not only absorbs, but the fact that it is colder necessarily condenses the warmer air, and as a result it receives all the impurities that fall. Housekeepers should, therefore, be careful not only to have the vessel covered when set out to receive the milk from the milkman, but they should be specially careful to keep the milk covered, whether it be in the larder, cellar, or kitchen.

I have thus referred to milk because I believe if the people better understood the difference between human and cow's milk, there would not be so much sickness, and the cow's milk and the milkman would not be so often blamed. The only tests that I rely upon outside of analyses are to obtain the volume of cream, which should be at the very least 12 per cent, then get the specific gravity of the milk after the cream has been taken off, which should be close to 1.036. Every household should be supplied with conveniences to make these tests. There is a little German patent tester that will test milk in a second to the satisfaction of almost any one. If milkmen knew that their customers are taking these precautions they will furnish good milk all the time.

Realizing that grass is the natural food for milch cows, and that the pasture is their home, I have made their changed condition a study, so that the milk supply should not become unhealthful either by reason of diseased cows, unwholesome foods, water, or air, ever bearing in mind that unwholesome air is far more dangerous to milk than the eating by cows of unwholesome food; for in the latter case digestion may overcome the impurities, while in the former, the air is taken into the lungs, and then to the blood, and milk being the direct product of the blood, would be sure to be impure.

Unfortunately my predecessor had instructed many dairymen to use lime, or chloride of lime, as a disinfectant, and they, like many others, not knowing that lime did the very thing they did not want done, were at a loss to know why their cow stables were so unpleasant. After explaining to them that lime set free the offensive matter, ammonia, etc., and that gypsum (land plaster) not only attracted but held the impurities, we have no trouble.

In this department of my duties I have had, free of expense, the kindly aid of Dr. James Withycombe, Oregon's worthy State veterinarian.

When I say the enforcement of the cubic-air provision of the law, giving each cow when stabled 800 feet of air, as well as prohibiting cows standing in their stables head to head unless there be an air-tight partition, and to see that cleanly surroundings were furnished, has worked wonders, I speak the truth.

In order to detect the adulteration of milk by the addition of water, or by the removal of cream, it becomes of great importance to determine whether the constituents of average milk vary between certain limits, and what these limits are. The constituents vary, more especially the fatty matter, according to age, breed, time before or after calving, the quantity of the food, condition of the animal, etc. But even taking into consideration these facts, we find that nature in its endeavor to produce a healthy food for the young will, in a great measure, overcome surroundings which are most antagonistic to the production of healthy normal milk. So much has been done to determine what the standard is below which pure, healthy milk never falls, that we now know with absolute certainty that the variation in the constituents of average milk is between certain defined limits. The milk of our cows is much better here than it is in the East. This fact is attributable to our richer food and equable climate.

I had 15 analyses made of our dairy milk, which averaged specific gravity 1.031; cream by volume, 15; sugar, 4.51; fat, 6.46; total solids, 14.51; solids not fat, 9.42; ash, 0.727; albumen, 3.63; 0.72 not traced. I have for my guide the following: 87.5 water, 3.2 fat, 9.3 solids not fat; total solids, 12.5.

Reliable authority reckons that one-half the people buy the butter and milk they consume, and that each person consumes 26 pounds of butter per annum. This tells us that the people of this State buy and consume annually 4,550,000 pounds of butter, which, at 30 cents per pound, aggregates $1,365,000.

The same good authority shows that half the people of this State would consume 7,971,500 gallons of milk, valued at $1,594,350; total butter and milk, $2,950,350. This exceeds the cash in all our banks; and when the value of the cows and implements are considered this industry exceeds any other one, even that of wheat.

Without desiring to accuse any class with whom I have had to deal since holding the office of food commissioner, I must in justice say that very many of the dairies when I commenced my work were in a deplorable condition. Quite a number of cows were ordered out, and by order of Dr. Withycombe, State veterinarian, 2 or 3 were killed. The fault lies in the fact that a large proportion of the milkmen are ignorant as to sanitary conditions. And, to me, the greatest work of our food law is, that it either forces or persuades milkmen to recognize such sanitary conditions as guarantee a healthful milk supply. And as the law of reversion is much swifter than that of progression, I anticipate that unless a watchful observance is kept up, most of the dairies would soon be as I found them.

A NATIONAL STANDARD FOR CHEESE.

Following is the address of W. S. Eberman, chemist to the Minnesota Dairy and Food Commission, delivered before the National Food and Dairy Commissioners' Association, held in Washington, D. C., in 1892:

The activity of some of the leading cheese-makers of Ohio at the first meeting of the National Dairy and Food Commissioners' Association will not soon be forgotten. Especially were we impressed with one of the manufacturers, Mr. Straight, a shrewd, clear-headed, well-poised business man. This gentleman declared that there were not in the entire State of Ohio 3 factories which made straight, full-cream cheese the season or the year through. Mr. Straight made what might be termed an attempt at a very able defense with reference to the manufacture of skim and part skim cheese. He took the position that it required less than all the butter fat which was in whole milk to make a good and palatable cheese.

At this point some exceedingly brisk firing commenced at short range. Hon. Hiram Smith, a veteran diaryman of Wisconsin, was there to fight for honest foods and honest dairy products. How nobly he defended the cause for which he had fought so long those of us who were there can bear proof. With Mr. Smith it was not what amount of fat could be taken out of this or that month's milk to make a fair palatable cheese of what was left. He said we could make no gauge for skimming out a certain amount of butter till we knew what there is of fat left in. What remains in and is actually incorporated in the cheese is what gives it its character. Here the keynote was struck, and as the several members took departure for home they were convinced that it paid in more ways than one to make the richest, purest, and most inviting cheese which the manufacturer was capable of producing.

A dairy product that has reached the enormous worth of $40,000,000 per annum in the United States needs to be carefully husbanded. The necessity of making whole-milk cheese can not be urged too strongly on our cheese-makers.

Prof. L. B. Arnold and Dr. Englehart made a series of experiments to test the digestibility of different makes of cheese. They found that the digestibility of whole-milk cheese, properly cured, depended on the amount of acids it contained. That which contained the least acid was the most digestible. That very much soured was the most indigestible.

Prof. Arnold also contended for the superiority of sweet cured cheese. His teachings rejected at home were gladly accepted by the Canadians; hence the superiority of Canadian cheese.

The meaty, mellow, rich-flavored cheddar is the cheese which most Americans prefer.

The American stands ready to adopt cheese as an important item of food as soon as the cheese-maker is ready to fulfill his share of the covenant. He must put the whole milk into the cheese. It has been fully demonstrated by the best cheese instructors of the United States that 6 and even 7 per cent of fat can be worked into the milk and coagulated by the rennet. Thus a rich, wholesome, perfect cheese is the resultant product.

Scientists and those who devote much attention to the relative value of different foods give cheese a prominent place. There is no food which contains a larger per cent of nutrition when properly made and properly cured, especially when the cheese contains the proper elements of milk, i. e., fat, etc.

Some of the unscrupulous dealers in our country have got hold of the export trade and have gone far towards ruining the market by palming off on foreigners a half-skimmed white-oak cheese which they can not find sale for at home. Is it not about time to call a halt and to insist on a change in the cheese business? Expose this species of dishonesty and adopt measures whereby the parties who practice deception may be brought to justice. To ask what shall be the national standard for cheese is apparently easy. However, it is not so readily answered. A quarter of a century ago we knew that a New York full-cream cheese was all that the brand implied. To-day the cheese branded New York full cream may, upon investigation, prove to be a skim-milk cheese, made of the rankest, rottenest kind of butter, lard, and other fats.

During the year 1887 the dairy commissioner of Minnesota deemed it advisable to have a standard fixed for cheese. There was no precedent to guide us, as no State in the Union had taken a step in that direction.

Data of a most satisfactory character were hard to obtain. It necessitated the taking of samples from each cheese factory in the State; also a large number of samples was gathered from the stores and markets of the different towns of the State. The next step was to secure data from other States in order to make comparison and to draw our conclusions.

By a careful study of our own work and a close examination of analyses of cheese furnished from other States we ascertained that a cheese well made, properly handled, and properly cured would not contain less than 40 per cent of fats to total solids. Some may ask, why not make the standard 30 per cent of fats to the entire amount, regardless of total solids. Many of the States have a standard of milk fixed at 3.50 per cent of fat. To have a less per cent of fat for cheese would result in a lowering of the milk standard, and, besides, it would work an injustice to consumers of milk.

Furthermore, it has been thoroughly demonstrated that a full-cream cheese well made, properly cured, and carefully handled until mature has about these constituents:

	Per cent.
Water	32
Fat	35
Casein	30
Ash	3
Total	100

During the past year we have had analyzed in our department 1,050 samples of cheese. Less than 5 per cent of the entire amount proved to be adulterated below our fixed standard, viz, 40 per cent of fat to total solids. The cheese of the State averaged nearly 50 per cent of fats to total solids.

It is safe to presume that the full-cream cheese of Wisconsin, Iowa, New York, New Jersey, Vermont, and Massachusetts will be found to contain as high an average per cent of fat as the full-cream cheese of Minnesota.

MILK STANDARDS.

No more important question arises than the quality of the milk used by the people, especially as upon its purity and strength depend the health and strength of the infants and life of invalids. The several States, cities, and larger towns have adopted laws relative to the sale of milk and regarding its purity. Some of the standards are given below. A very fair standard to the seller would be as follows:

	Per cent.
Total solids	12.5
Fat	3.25

and such milk can be relied upon as healthy and pure.

The board of health of Nashville, Tenn., is authorized to inspect and test the milk sold in that city, and if it fall below the standard they may "cause official publication of the fact to be made in the city press." This board of health requires as a standard:

	Per cent.
Milk solids	12.5
Water	87.5

Vermont, as shown in the report of the experiment station of that State for 1888 (p. 142), requires the following standard:

	Per cent.
Total solids	12.5
Fat	3.25

except in May and June, when the following is the standard:

	Per cent.
Total solids	12.0
Fat	3.0

Oregon, as shown in the food commissioners' report for 1893 (p. 95), requires the following standard:

	Per cent.
Water	87.5
Fat	3.2
Solids other than fat	9.3
Total solids	12.5

Iowa, by act of the twenty-fourth general assembly, requires 3 pounds of butter fat to the 100 pounds of milk.

New York, in its dairy law, chapter 202, section 8, requires 12 per cent of solids, and 25 per cent of such solids, or 3 per cent of the milk, shal be fat.

Ohio, in section 4 of an act to amend section 4, found in vol. 86, p. 229, 230, says:

Not more than 87 per cent watery fluid nor less than 12.5 per cent solids, not less than one-fourth of which must be fat.

Wisconsin requires not less than 3 per cent of butter fat in milk.

Prof. P. Vieth, of the British Society of Public Analysts, for the eleven years inclusive of 1881–1891, examined 120,540 samples of milk, and found an average of constituent parts as follows:

	Per cent.
Total solids	12.09
Fat	4.01
Solids not fat	8.8

(*See* p. 664, Mass. Report for 1891.)

In the Massachusetts Health Report for 1891 (p. 664), an analysis shows 13.2 to 13.3 per cent of total solids, and the same report gives this standard: Solids (except in May and June), 13 per cent; for May and June, 12 per cent.

Dr. Abbott, secretary of the Massachusetts State Board of Health, after quoting the analysis of Prof. Vieth, says:

As a general rule, the figures presented by Prof. Vieth show that milk of the first half of the year was slightly below, and that of the last half slightly above, the yearly average. In commenting upon the effect of seasons upon milk, the same writer says:

"A bad season for haymaking is, in my experience, almost invariably followed by a particularly low depression in the quality of milk toward the end of winter. Should the winter be of unusual severity and length, the depression will be still more marked. Long spells of cold and wet, as well as of heat and drought, during the time when cows are kept on pasture, also unfavorably influence the quality, and, I may add, the quantity, of milk."

The foregoing remarks have reference only to milk as regarded from the standpoint of chemical analysis. To a certain extent this view of the subject has a bearing upon the public health, since the addition of water to milk, or the abstraction of cream, impairs its quality as nutriment in proportion to the extent of the adulteration. Strangely enough, the pretense is often urged by milk producers that milk containing 11 or 12 per cent of total solids is quite as wholesome or nutritious as that which contains 13 or 14 per cent of solids. The absurdity of this argument is plain enough, since, if it were true, it might reasonably be asserted that milk having 7 or 8 per cent of solids is as wholesome as that which has 11 per cent, and so on *ad infinitum*.

FOOD LEGISLATION AND FOREIGN TRADE.

If proper legislation is adopted, without extending too much the army of office-holders or interfering too much with private enterprise, it will be of benefit in extending our foreign trade.—*American Analyst.*

MAXIMUM WATER ALLOWABLE IN BUTTER.

The following is an extract from the proceedings of the Public Analysts, found in the London (England) Analyst for March, 1893:

During the discussion Mr. Allen said that he had very strongly laid down in the witness box and elsewhere that 15 per cent was the maximum quantity of water to be allowed in butter, which could be raised to 16 per cent as an outside figure. He thought a rigid line should be drawn at 16 per cent and he believed that if that were done there would be very little difficulty in reducing the quantity of water in commercial butters to that amount. Some people could, no doubt, be found who would excuse even 35 or 40 per cent, and an inspector from the Cork butter market recently stated on oath that the proportion of water in the butter depended on the atmospheric conditions at the time the cows were milked. Similarly, Dr. Bell has recently stated that he did not see his way to regard butter as adulterated if it did not contain more water than had been known to be left in it when not manufactured for sale. This seemed to him to be practically making an incompetent dairy maid the referee under the food act.

Mr. Helmer agreed that 15 per cent was a reasonable and liberal figure for water allowance. Butter fresh from the dairy, however, contained more water than butter which had been packed and transported to market.

LABELING PRODUCTS TRUTHFULLY.

Mr. F. N. Barrett, editor of the American Grocer, under date of March 27, 1893, says:

I more than ever cling to the principle enunciated to you some time ago, that food laws should be simple and compel the sale of every thing for what it is, and then leave the consumer perfectly free to buy anything he wishes. I think it should be the province of the food commissioner to strengthen confidence in the integrity of the food supply rather than create distrust by reporting suspected articles. A great hue and cry is made over adulterated spices, but when one considers the quantity of spice used by any one individual as compared with the total amount of food consumed it is a mere bagatelle. Another thing—inspectors are apt to gather only samples of suspected food, and when a large proportion of these are found to be adulterated, it seems to appear a more glaring evil than it really is. For instance, there is carried on in the city of Philadelphia the manufacture of imitation coffee beans, molded to the shape of the roasted berry, but composed wholly of matter foreign to coffee beans. The proportion of such stuff sold to the total amount of coffee consumed is scarcely worthy of notice, and yet such a hue and cry is raised over the few bogus beans sold as to create the impression that the coffee supply is terribly adulterated.

With the Department of Agriculture on record as indorsing oleomargarin as a wholesome and valuable food product, it seems strange to find the food commissioners of the various States carrying on a vigorous crusade against the article and denouncing its venders in terms more fitting criminals than merchants in honorable trade. We must bear in mind that there are a great many articles sold that are classed as adulterations which are perfectly harmless and valuable as food products. For instance, the German prefers his coffee mixed with chicory or with the addition of a slight proportion of caramel. There is nothing objectionable in this, and yet this product is condemned. The only point is that the mixture should be sold for what it is and then the responsibility rests with the consumer, who in case of injury has a remedy at law.

○